Facilities in sports
and physical education

Facilities in sports and physical education

EUGENE M. EZERSKY, B.S., M.A., Ed.D.

Coordinator, Bureau for Health and Physical Education,
New York City Board of Education; Consultant, Educational
Facilities Laboratories, Inc.; formerly Associate Professor of
Education, New York University, New York, New York

P. RICHARD THEIBERT, B.A., M.A.

Assistant to the President, William Woods College,
Fulton, Missouri; Consultant, Educational Facilities
Laboratories, Inc., New York, New York

with 163 illustrations

The C. V. Mosby Company

Saint Louis   1976

Library of Congress Cataloging in Publication Data

Ezersky, Eugene.
    Facilities in sports and physical education.

    Bibliography: p.
    1.   Physical education facilities.   I.   Theibert,
P. Richard, joint author.   II.   Title.
GV401.E93   301.5'7   75-46556
ISBN 0-8016-1534-8

GW/CB/B   9   8   7   6   5   4   3   2   1

Foreword

These are vivid times. Cultures are colliding, priorities are being reordered, life-styles are changing, and everywhere our institutions are on the defensive.

Just as education as an institution is feeling the pressures of the times, each of its elements is being challenged. Because health, physical education, and recreation involve the whole person, this field has been more sensitive to changing demands than have the more academic pursuits. Indeed, physical education and athletics have provided entry for the earliest applications of innovation and reform in education: coaches were usually first to employ instructional technology—the overhead projector and micro-teaching through film and instant playback. The use of teacher aides and paraprofessionals has long been a natural staffing pattern in physical education, sports, and recreation.

Physical educators have every right to be proud of their profession. Looking back over the years, physical education as a systemic body of knowledge has not only been sensitive to constructive change, but has withstood the ravages of economic pressure, although often the target, along with art, music, guidance, and the so-called nonacademic subjects, whenever budget cutting became the order of the day.

Looking to the future, all physical educators will be challenged from every quarter to justify their programs and the costs of physical facilities required to accommodate those programs. Educators everywhere are being asked three questions:

1. What are you doing?
2. Why are you doing it?
3. Why are you doing it that way?

The experience of Messrs. Ezersky and Theibert in helping education at all levels, public and private, to find better ways of helping persons of all ages to engage in healthful activities should be invaluable to students and practitioners in the field. Aside from the authors' extensive involvement in educational planning from coast to coast and in numerous foreign countries, each possesses a unique inquisitiveness that often reveals the shape of things to come in matters physical. They sense the trends before the trends become the fashion.

This book lays out in informal, readable style the kinds of considerations the authors and their colleagues bring to bear on the problems emerging in the field. For health, physical education, and recreation, Ezersky and Theibert's *Facilities in Sports and Physical Education* is a kind of early-warning system.

Harold B. Gores, *President*
Educational Facilities Laboratories, Inc.
New York, New York

Preface

This book offers the reader some options and alternatives for building facilities for physical education and recreation based on a conceptualization of what ought to be built and what can be built. We do not intend for this book to tell very much about how to build. This is best left to the professionals in the building trades—the architects and construction engineers. Neither do we suggest what to build, since this should be an institutional decision reflecting the needs and finances of a particular community. Rather, we wish to present some philosophical principles that we hope will mold the *how* and *what* into a perspective that will create facilities which are technically feasible, programmatically utilitarian, reasonably priced, and aesthetically pleasing.

A word should be said here about the aggregate of experiences that goes into this volume. Over the past twenty years, we have had experience at every level of teaching and administering programs of physical education and sports. This includes teaching, coaching, and serving as athletic directors in secondary schools and colleges. It also includes considerable experience in public recreation and in the management of sports arenas and facilities.

Nevertheless, it was the advent of our association with Educational Facilities Laboratories, Inc., a nonprofit corporation established in 1958 by the Ford Foundation to help schools and colleges with their physical problems, that projected us headlong into grappling with the problems of athletic facilities. As consultants to EFL for recreation and physical education since 1967, we have been privileged to be associated with a group who have been on the cutting edge of facility innovation, one whose concepts and professional expertise have generally earned them a reputation as the acknowledged leaders in educational facility planning. EFL has been an early-warning system for educational change, and their reports on so diverse a range of educational facilities as college libraries, environmental education resources, open-plan schools, and community schools have been well received and widely circulated. As consultants for EFL, we have had occasion to travel widely to see people who were confronting peculiar facility problems. We have had the opportunity to be associated with projects where innovative and remarkable achievements crowned the efforts of equally innovative and remarkable people at all levels of education. Similarly, we had the chance to observe firsthand the frustrations and waste that result from poorly planned and ill-conceived facilities.

Perhaps the biggest impact on our thinking came as the result of our association with Dr. Harold B. Gores, president of EFL, whose thoughts on educational facilities have been translated into some of the most architecturally daring, aesthetically pleasing, and educationally utilitarian facilities in the country. He served as an astute sounding board for our ideas—probing, questioning, cajoling, encouraging. The depth of his thoughts was hidden in the simple yardstick by which he measured all his and our projects, "Is it good for kids?" Our indebtedness and gratitude to him for his inspiration and help in cementing our professional thoughts and careers can never fully be expressed. Indeed, the whole EFL staff responded so generously, professionally, and frequently to our requests that we suspect our readers will not object to our mentioning them by name: Alan C. Green, Peter Green, Larry Molloy, Frances Shaw, Danae Voltos, Mary Webb, Ruth Weinstock, Gwen Frederickson, Beryl Fields, Margaret Nyhus, Wendell Williams, Rhoda Kraus, and Lyn Smith, among others.

Additionally, we state our gratitude to James Fullerton and Dr. Milton A. Gabrielsen for contributing chapters to this text and similarly acknowledge our thanks to Susan Smith and Renee Nankin for their assistance in getting the manuscript in order.

Finally, our very warm and personal acknowledgments to our wives, Myrna and Ann, and to our children, whose "lives with father" were considerably disrupted during the years of preparation of this text.

Eugene M. Ezersky

P. Richard Theibert

Contents

CHAPTER 1

Historical antecedents and sociological trends in physical education and recreation

THE LEISURE REVOLUTION

The United States is undergoing a leisure revolution that many sociologists and economists believe will make the Industrial Revolution pale by comparison in its effect on the daily lives of individuals.

A conservative estimate puts the current recreation market at upward of $150 billion a year—approximately 15% of the gross national product—and it is growing.

In 1970 we spent $516 million on spectator sports. Horse racing attracted 71 million enthusiasts; auto racing, 41 million; football games, 38 million; baseball, 37 million; basketball, 27 million. Seventy million swimmers used our waters or the grounds near-by, 42 million bowlers rolled their balls down 215,000 lanes; 32 million fishermen cast their lures; 18 million hunters stalked their game and each other; 12 million golfers swung their clubs on 9,000 courses and 75 million pairs of legs pedalled bicycles.*

The enormous growth of participation in recreational sports in the 1970s is evidenced in an A. C. Nielsen Company survey that showed dramatic increases in participation in such activities as swimming, boating, bicycling, fishing, camping, and bowling. In reporting on this survey, the *New York Times* stated: "Tennis, once a sport for the classes, finally appears to have reached the masses and now is more popular than golf with women. Over twenty million Americans 'play' tennis according to the Nielsen projection estimates."[4] There are at least 13 million regular tennis players in the country and almost as many golfers.

A 1973 national survey by the National Federation of State High School Associations reported two significant trends.[3] First, "Virtually all schools now include a goodly number of non-income producing sports." Since the non-income-producing sports are generally the leisure-time or lifetime sports, this strongly suggests adult carry-over (Fig. 1-1). The second trend is the "great increase in interscholastic programs for girls." Already a tremendous number of women actively participate in regular programs of tennis, bowling, golf, skiing, jogging, and swimming, and more can be expected. The landmark Title IX decision of the 1972 United States Education Amendments dramatically punctuated the progress that women have made in striving for the fullest benefits of sports and athletic participation.

---

*From Ensign, William L.: The American endless weekend, The AIA Journal, p. 19, Sept., 1972.

1

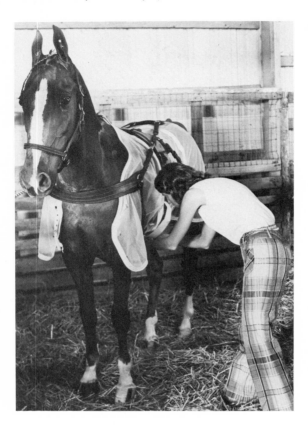

Fig. 1-1. William Woods College equestrian recreation program in Fulton, Missouri.

According to the noted philosopher and futurist, R. Buckminster Fuller: "Health, physical education and recreation (HYPER) may play a far more critical part in the lives of coming generations than such educational system disciplines have played in the past."[1]

What are the factors that contribute to this new and growing interest in physical participation? A recital of them only serves to underscore the totality with which the United States has been engulfed in this revolution of activity.

1. The leisure ethic is quickly replacing the work ethic as a desirable form of human endeavor. It is no longer taboo to have fun. Quite the contrary, it is desirable. No longer does the company executive sneak off to play golf. He revels in it as do the people who work for him and who frequently play with him. It is "in" to play.

Partly responsible for this new positive attitude toward leisure is the public's heightened awareness of the importance of physical fitness. When President Dwight D. Eisenhower suffered a serious heart attack in 1955, his physician, noted cardiologist Paul Dudley White, insisted that he continue to play golf during and after his recuperation, a popularization of a change in medical opinion as to how postcardiac conditions should be treated. White turned national attention to the fact that the human body requires physical activity at all

Fig. 1-2. Herman's World of Sporting Goods, Garden City, New York.
(Photo by Peter Ezersky.)

stages of life, that the trouble with aging is not that people grow old, but rather that they grow inactive. The Kennedy years glamourized physical activity and sports; the "in thing" was to participate in challenge and adventure.

2. *The United States is built on an economy that promotes mobility.* Americans are on the move in millions of autos and recreational vehicles. Americans fly more than 4 billion miles a year. Although not all of this is for recreational pursuits, the mobility syndrome is a reality, and there is little doubt that Americans travel extensively for pleasure. Whereas the office secretary of

3

twenty years ago hoped at best for a two-week vacation at the nearby seashore or mountains, today's mammoth jets, the energy crisis notwithstanding, carry these same secretaries all over the world for fun and relaxation at affordable prices and in vacation time periods of the same two weeks or more. Sports activities that were formerly unavailable to most metropolitan area dwellers are now within easy reach. Swimming, surfing, sailing, scuba diving, water skiing —the sun sports—are now common recreational pursuits of every segment of American society. Similarly, the remarkable increase in American skiers can be traced directly to their ability to get to some of the best slopes in the world within just a few hours. Although energy shortages do have an effect on this mobility, there is little doubt that recreational travel will continue, through environmentally sound and energy-conserving means promoted and regulated by government policy.

3. *Economic factors have greatly contributed to the new upswing in physical activity.* Social security benefits have been increased, and with other retirement benefits accruing from pension plans and union packages, the elderly have become active participants in leisure and sports programs rather than mere spectators. Earlier retirement has added significant numbers to the "play force." For those still actively employed, the four-day week, longer vacations, group travel plans, and company-sponsored recreation programs have generated increased interest in recreation, with resulting increased participation.

As leisure activity grows, the leisure industry also grows, contributing a greater share to the gross national product (Fig. 1-2). Additional manufacturing plants for ski equipment, boats, and tennis equipment, together with the tremendous growth in the travel industry, are just some examples of this force in action. Whole new industries have emerged because of what leisure activities have generated.

HISTORICAL DEVELOPMENT OF PHYSICAL EDUCATION IN U.S. SCHOOLS

Physical education, like any discipline of education, responds to the needs and movements of the times. Until as late as 1930 American education reflected the traditional and formalized character of its European models, and physical education was also very formal. Activities featured mass synchronized drills, formal Swedish and German calisthenics, and coordinated rhythms (Fig. 1-3).

Beginning after World War I and continuing to the early 1970s competitive team sports grew at a rapid pace for boys and young men in the educational system. A by-product could be seen when leagues were organized for children as young as 6 years of age on a national and international level. In the 1970s a similar growth of and emphasis on women's teams at all levels has been witnessed as Title IX became law.

During both world wars, physical education in the United States reacted swiftly to the national need for physical fitness for military service. Crash programs were organized involving obstacle courses, stamina runs, combative ac-

Fig. 1-3. Physical education took on many different characteristics as times changed. (Photos courtesy American Alliance for Health, Physical Education and Recreation.)

tivities, and self-defense. Any physical activity programs that reduced the number of rejections for the military draft were considered "highly successful."

When the United States began to move toward a more leisure-oriented society after World War II, programs developing lifetime sports came into vogue. Individual sports such as golf, tennis, and skiing were advocated, skills that would contribute to a lifetime of active physical participation. During the Eisenhower and Kennedy administrations the President's Council on Physical

5

Fig. 1-4. The Appalachian Trail and other outdoor sites all over the country serve as learning resources for thousands of American schoolchildren. (Photo by Jane Ezersky.)

Fitness and Sports became the national clearinghouse for programs leading to fitness.

The informal openness of American education in the 1960s saw changes affecting traditional programs of physical education. Changing life-styles of American youth were reflected in physical education programs. The popular "open" elementary classrooms of the 1960s were accompanied by equally informal and loosely structured programs of physical education.

In addition, young people responded massively to activity programs in natural outdoor surroundings; hiking, backpacking, and mountaineering reflected the keen interest in the environmental movement that swept the country (Fig. 1-4).

The extent to which "open" education has affected physical education programs is dramatically illustrated by the New York City Board of Education's curriculum guide entitled "Options in Physical Education for High Schools."[2] Camping, hiking, cycling, archery, roller skating and ice skating, casting, camp counseling, exploring, and wilderness survival were strongly advocated by educators of the largest inner city in the country. Essential to this alternative education "is the awareness of the classroom outside the school." The guide clearly makes a case for utilizing the larger community's resources and facilities. A multitude of facilities can be found outside the four walls of the traditional schoolhouse, as subsequent chapters in this text will show.

REFERENCES

1. Fuller, R. Buckminster: HYPER—a concept for an integrated physical education facility, World, p. 38, April 10, 1973.
2. Options in physical education for high schools, New York, 1973, Bureau of Curriculum Development, New York City Board of Education.
3. Sports Participation Survey of the National Federation of State High School Associations, Elgin, Ill., April, 1973.
4. Swimming still rated top participant sport; camping on increase, The New York Times, March 24, 1974.

CHAPTER 2

Facility considerations and new trends for today's physical education

Those considering educational or recreational facilities construction would do well to familiarize themselves with some of the realities of life in the United States in the mid-1970s. The Annual Education Review of the *New York Times* succinctly expressed the state of the education art in its headline story entitled, "Education '74: Sober Realism and Cautious Hope."[3] What are some of these realities and where do we look for hope?

THE ECONOMICS OF EDUCATION

It is not an exaggeration to say that many educational institutions face bankruptcy, and the financial condition of most school systems has led to enforced austerity. Private colleges and universities are generally in difficult financial straits. The cost of building, salaries, supplies, and every ingredient of education has risen in line with the inflationary spiral that has gripped the country. The cost of borrowing money, of union and retirement benefits, and of every category of personnel and educational support has risen accordingly. The National Center for Educational Statistics and the National Education Association reported that expenditure per pupil for education in the United States increased 138.7% in the 1960s and that teacher salaries increased almost 80%. This kind of statistical analysis supports what all administrators know: the cost of educational services is exploding.

Federal and state funds, so long taken for granted by the educational establishment, have been drastically cut, and the voters are defeating school bond issues with regularity. The result has been a reduction of many school offerings and services and the certain elimination of frills and luxuries.

POPULATION CHANGES

Population projections for the coming decades are critical in planning for educational facilities. Concern about population growth, the availability of birth control, and other factors have resulted in a leveling off of the birth rate in the United States. Many school systems now find themselves "shrinking their school system." Elementary schools that sprang up in the 1950s to accommodate the war babies now stand idle. Since the budgets of many schools are determined by enrollment-based formulas, the declining enrollment growth in the seventies and eighties will mean diminished resources. Many school administrators are already grappling with the problem of what to do with unused school buildings. By 1974, the pages of many professional educational journals contained information on how to close down schools. A major study of this problem conducted by the Educational Facilities Laboratories was reported in "Fewer Pupils/Surplus Space."[4] At the other end of the population scale is a growing number of older people. This prompts the question of what should be done to meet the requirements of the elder segment of the population.

Not only are population levels changing, but population centers are also shifting. Urban dwellers have moved further out from the core of the central cities, and the vacated elementary schools in closer-in communities are now needed further out in suburbia. As the babies in exurbia grow up, the shift in facility needs will pass from elementary to middle to senior school. To the wise, therefore, this suggests a very fluid approach to school facilities.

NEW TRENDS IN EDUCATION

Trends in American education—schools without walls, the peripatetic student, alternative schools, community-based education—all involve education away from the school. Authorities believe it is possible and even desirable to teach away from the desk and the four walls of the classroom, and they also advocate using the things and the people around them as sources for learning. *In physical education, with the proliferation of recreational facilities springing up all around, this concept is particularly valid. Shared facilities for physical education are almost mandated.*

Increasingly, therefore, school systems are seeking partners for many of their operations. This trend is generated in part by economics, in part by philosophy, and in part by an attempt to reach out to the community where real life experiences can be offered.

HOPE FOR THE FUTURE
The community school movement

Some educators believe that the impact of the community school movement in the United States may be the most significant event in public education during the 1970s. Unlike the concept of the community school in the past, where the schoolhouse was open to the community for physical and cultural activities after school hours, the new community school is a place planned and operated cooperatively by schools and other social agencies twenty-four hours a day. "Economically, school districts can no longer afford to operate buildings for less than one third of the day for one half the year."[3]

Education and recreation facilities lend themselves easily to this cooperative concept, and those charged with the responsibility of developing facilities for sports should consider seriously the advantages of seeking others to share the expenses of construction and operation.

There are enough community school models in operation or in advanced stages of planning to be supportive of those who are ready to initiate building programs of this nature. The Thomas Jefferson Junior High School and Community Center in Arlington County, Virginia, is one of the best examples of this movement (Fig. 2-1). The school district, in cooperation with the Parks and Recreation Division of the Department of Environmental Affairs, was able to afford a far better combined community/school/recreation center than either agency could have built separately.

Continued.

Fig. 2-1. The Thomas Jefferson Junior High School and Community Center, Arlington, Virginia, serves the school and community in many ways. (Photos courtesy Educational Facilities Laboratories, Inc.)

Fig. 2-1, cont'd. For legend see p. 9.

Together the two agencies designed and produced an extraordinary facility which contained three district architectural features that would not have been possible if they had not combined forces:

1. a full community recreation center including game room, canteen, dining common, and a clubroom large enough for simultaneous use by both the community and students
2. a 730-seat theater capable of being subdivided into four discrete spaces lending itself to a variety of instructional purposes
3. a 68,000 square feet field house with air conditioning, multiuse surfacing and lighting capable of being adapted to levels suitable for television*

This Thomas Jefferson facility, along with forty-two other cooperatively utilized facilities in the district, recorded 98,171 hours of community recreation programs as compared to 64,984 hours for regular school use. Joseph Ringers, Jr., Assistant Superintendent of the Arlington, Virginia, public schools, stated that "The community is getting ample return on its investment as it is using the facilities one and a half times more hours than the students."[2]

In Gulf Breeze, Florida, an elementary school, junior high school, and senior high school were constructed on a sixty-acre site. None of the schools had any recreation or leisure facilities. Instead, a combination school and city sports complex was developed in the center of the three schools, including

---

*From Community/school: sharing the space and the action, New York, 1973, Educational Facilities Laboratories, p. 34.

Fig. 2-2. Several community agencies, as well as the gymnasium and auditorium, are housed in this building of the John F. Kennedy School and Community Center in Atlanta, Georgia. (Photo courtesy Educational Facilities Laboratories, Inc.; Larry Molloy, photographer.)

gymnasiums, indoor tennis courts, club and kitchen facilities, lounges, and a swimming pool. This school/civic center complex will be managed and financed jointly by the school district and the department of parks and recreation.

The John F. Kennedy School and Community Center in Atlanta, Georgia, is still another example of sensible recreational and educational planning. The center houses a school and many community recreational services under one roof and will include an enclosed swimming pool and public park for school and community use. (See Fig. 2-2.)

The list of advantages of shared facilities is long: in addition to shared construction costs, there are savings in acreage requirements, maintenance, and security and professional personnel.

Centralized facilities

We suggested a rather radical approach to developing new physical education facilities for urban and suburban communities in 1969. The proposal focused around the development of centralized facilities for use *by many schools*, as well as by the community in general. Although there has not been a major movement in this direction, there are beginning to be signs that the idea might be catching on. By 1974, the New York City Board of Education was actively planning for the construction of centralized sports arenas to accommodate major interscholastic spectator events on a borough-wide and county-wide basis.

Simply stated, the concept of centralized facilities suggests that, particularly in urban areas, rather than build the usual spectator-oriented physical education courts and fields in every new high school, economically it is more feasible to build a series of specialized centralized facilities that would serve all the schools in that area for their interscholastic programs. When one considers that almost 25% of the building cost of any new high school goes for the physical education plant, it becomes clear that by eliminating all but the basic practice and service course facility requirements in these new schools, the savings in cost can be considerable. These funds can then be used to build one centralized field for football/soccer/baseball activities and other specialized facilities for the racket games, aquatics, etc. It is our opinion that one result will be an improvement in the quality of the physical education program as well. In addition, possibilities of fee and rental programs for these facilities suggest even more economy of utilization, as well as making a significant contribution to the school and community recreation program.

A full analysis of the centralized field concept is given in the April, 1970, issue of the *Journal for Health and Physical Education.*[1]

Partnerships should be sought in building public sports facilities

Physical education professionals should be aware of the movement toward community schools. With the leveling off in birth rates, shifts in population, and financial difficulties besetting the country, it does not make sense to build just for schools, just for recreation, or just for the young or the old. If schools should be places of learning for all people, sports and recreation facilities should serve the entire local population as well. Shared building costs, shared maintenance costs, and shared personnel costs are the kinds of interagency cooperation that can provide better services for all. The various governmental agencies in the community that deal with education, social services for the young and aging, health care, recreation, and the cultural arts are all potential partners in providing good facilities for sports and physical education and should be actively encouraged to pursue this common goal.

Found spaces, joint occupancy, and conversion

School systems have converted theaters, catering halls, churches and synagogues, supermarkets, and bowling alleys to educational facilities (Figs. 2-3 to 2-5). They have leased space in commercial office buildings and in high-rise commercial buildings on either a long-range or short-term basis. They have operated schools in factories and literally have backed up vans to empty lofts, emptied a "supermarket" of educational tools, and created an instant school. Why? Because these spaces can be converted cheaply and quickly into places of learning. (See Figs. 2-6 to 2-9.)

Did you ever think you would see tennis courts on rooftops (Fig. 2-10) or abandoned piers, or a school sharing a high-rise tower with commercial office space and elegant apartments? It is possible to look down from the twenty-sixth floor of a high-rise tower at a varsity soccer game being played on a beautiful green surface below. The fact that the field is on top of a roof or a school, that the green surface is artificial grass, and that it is located in the middle of one of New York City's busiest industrial centers is indicative of the ingenuity of school and community planners. All these things are happening, and, what is more, they just scratch the surface of the potential of this concept. If you need better facilities for your physical education program, and if cost is a factor (it always is), remember that there may be several ways to skin the facility cat besides constructing something new. These ways may often be quicker and less expensive and might even mean a better place for your program. Frequently, too, it is the only viable solution to what otherwise might mean no facility at all.

A very successful complex of tennis court bubbles exists on two abandoned piers protruding out into New York City's East River, less than a five-minute walk from the heart of New York's teeming financial district (Fig. 2-11). Similarly, the "dead space" underneath the Queensborough Bridge, formerly a litter-strewn, inaccessible, irregularly shaped blight on the Manhattan landscape, was converted into a plush tennis club by some creative promoters and designers (Fig. 2-12). Rooftops, vacant lots, and parking spaces in shopping centers have all had recreational facilities built on them. The air rights over buildings and the rights to land under elevated highways have been used for similar purposes. Again, the possibilities are limitless for using these "found

Fig. 2-3. A lavishly decorated theater was converted into the gymnasium for Long Island University's Brooklyn Center. (Photo by Hugh Rogers.)

Fig. 2-4. Harlem Preparatory School is located in what once was a local supermarket. (Photo courtesy Educational Facilities Laboratories, Inc.)

spaces"; those entrusted with providing facilities should seriously consider this option, particularly where land is either expensive or scarce.

Stated simply, joint occupancy is an arrangement in which two or more agencies use the same facility, sharing the costs and sometimes the staff and other services. For many years, churches have housed many forms of social services for their congregations, and in the late 1960s more sophisticated forms of this practice came into being. By enactment of a special educational construction fund, New York City began to build schools on the lower floors of high-rise commercial office buildings, so that both school and commerce benefit from services and from new tax base arrangements. Joint occupancy lends itself particularly well to sports and recreation facilities, where the schools can use much needed facilities during school hours, and the public can avail themselves of much needed community recreation facilities before and after school hours. The full details of the joint occupancy concept can be found in a 1970 publication called "Joint Occupancy."[4]

All over the country examples abound of turning old theaters into gymnasiums, transforming lofts in commercial buildings into schools and play areas, and creating bowling alleys out of gyms and theaters and schools out of churches and synagogues. Old schools become museums, hotels, bakeries, recreation centers, or industrial plants, among other uses. Unused railroad stations have been converted to schools, cultural centers, banks, and restaurants. Precedent has been established. There may very well be all shapes and sizes of available facilities in your community that could easily be converted into topnotch physical education space easily and reasonably inexpensively.

15

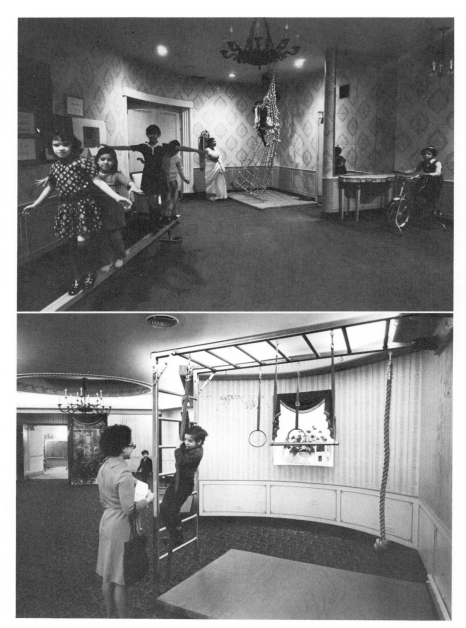

Fig. 2-5. The Burnside Elementary School in the Bronx, New York, previously was the site of elegant receptions and social functions.

Fig. 2-6. Vacant airplane hangars now house some of the facilities of Nassau Community College in New York.

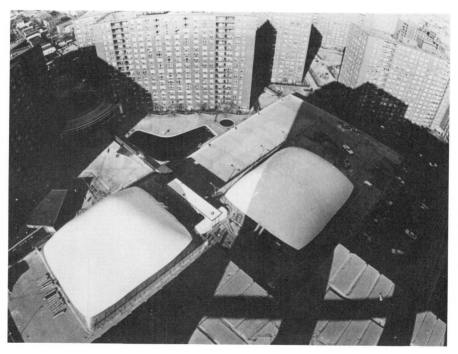

Fig. 2-7. Tennis atop garages in the heart of Lefrak City in New York. (Photos courtesy Air-Tech Industries, Inc.)

Fig. 2-8. Railroad stations convert to educational use, such as this Head Start program in Oberlin, Ohio. (Photo by William Wynne.)

A

Fig. 2-9. Exterior, **A,** and interior, **B,** views of the unused Los Angeles Union Station indicate the large open areas suitable for recreational purposes. (Photos courtesy Santa Fe Railway.)

B

Fig. 2-9, cont'd. For legend see opposite page.

Fig. 2-10. Rooftop tennis at Portland State University, Portland, Oregon.

Fig. 2-11. Unused piers in the East River at the foot of Wall Street in New York's financial district now house lush facilities for tennis. (Photo courtesy Air-Tech Industries, Inc., and The Wall Street Racquet Club.)

Multiuse concept of physical education facilities

The multiuse concept of physical education facilities is another trend of the 1970s. Building for one purpose no longer suffices. Notre Dame's $8.6 million Athletic Convocation Center (Fig. 2-13) is perhaps the best example of this trend. Two domed structures provide enough flexibility so that one dome can be converted into a basketball arena seating 11,000 or an auditorium seating about 12,000 for stage shows and concerts. The other dome focuses on track and field and ice rink sports. It includes a ten-lap synthetic track, three superimposed tennis courts, two batting cages, a baseball infield, and an ice facility.

Fig. 2-12. "Dead space" under New York's Queensborough Bridge was converted into a plush tennis club.

Fig. 2-13. Notre Dame's Athletic Convocation Center.

Hofstra University in Nassau County, New York, worked out an arrangement to provide the New York Jets with an on-campus training facility (Fig. 2-14). The university donated the land and constructed the building and grounds. In return the Jets reimbursed the university for all capital costs and took over the facility for a period of ten years. Afterward the entire complex becomes the property of Hofstra University. During this period, however, the school may use the facility when the pros do not need it.

Fig. 2-14. The New York Jets' building on the campus of Hofstra University. Taller building in rear is Hofstra's Physical Education Center. (Photo by Peter Ezersky.)

Fig. 2-15. Full range of collegiate and community events takes place in the enclosed stadium of Idaho State University, Pocatello, Idaho. (Photos courtesy Cedric M. Allen and Tom H. Myers, architects.)

Fig. 2-15, cont'd. For legend see opposite page. *Continued.*

Fig. 2-15, cont'd. For legend see p. 22.

Fig. 2-16. A, Shelter at Riverside Elementary School in Princeton Township, New Jersey, covers a play area of 49 by 80 feet. **B,** Shelters make ideal seasonal sports facilities such as this gymnastics facility at Trail's End Camp in Beach Lake, Pennsylvania. (**A** courtesy Gruzen & Partners, architects; **B** courtesy Joseph Laub.)

An outstanding example of the multiuse concept and encapsulation of large space was the construction of the first enclosed stadium on a university campus at Idaho State University in Pocatello, Idaho (Fig. 2-15). The building is a steel barrel vault with closed ends.

Shelters for physical education and recreation

An inexpensive and practical way to provide additionally needed facilities is by using shelters. Shelters are no more than coverings that give a physical boundary to space and protect it from the elements. In some cases, shelters take the form of roofs and sides, in some cases just a roof alone, and in other cases merely siding alone. Rigid materials are generally used, although shelters can be fashioned from shrubs and trees, depending on the direction of the prevailing winds and the position of the sun. (See Fig. 2-16.)

Additional ideas on possibilities of sharing costs and services for physical education facilities can be gained from other publications of Educational Facilities Laboratories.[4]

REFERENCES

1. City schools without gyms, Journal for Health and Physical Education 41:26, April, 1970.
2. Co-op facility shows big community usage, American School and University, p. 16, Sept., 1973.
3. Education '74: Sober realism and cautious hope, New York Times, Jan. 16, 1974.
4. Educational Facilities Laboratories, Inc., 850 Third Ave., New York, N.Y. 10022:
   Community/school: sharing the space and the action, 1973
   Fewer pupils/surplus space, 1974
   Generating revenues from college facilities, 1974
   Joint occupancy, 1970
   Physical recreation facilities, 1973
   Places and things for experimental schools, 1972

CHAPTER 3

Planning for facilities

Today's problems should challenge the thinking of anyone considering building a facility. An open mind and alertness to changing situations and innovative solutions are crucial. In addition, the general state of the art in education and architecture also contributes to the end product. Therefore an examination of some broad planning concepts is in order.

MAJOR CONCEPTS TO THINK ABOUT BEFORE STARTING

1. Don't be the last of the old. It's better to be the first of the new. There is a "play it safe" syndrome in the design of schools and other public buildings. Everyone jumps on the bandwagon to be second, but the dangers and mistakes inherent in being first understandably make people reluctant to pioneer new concepts in facility construction. It is much easier to make a slightly better copy of a facility that is already up. However, buildings have a way of becoming obsolete almost before they are completed, and it is important not to be such a traditional copycat that your building is considered old before it is occupied.

There are advantages to being first (Fig. 3-1). If you make mistakes, they are usually excused because your facility was the first of its kind. Also, a facility that is functional and also promotes a new technology is immediately the object of much publicity, usually good. This exposure may attract funds for evaluation and research. Frequently, manufacturers are willing to offer reductions in cost to provide visibility for their products. Members of the professional staff find themselves sought after as speakers and resource people for others who are interested in similar facilities. Although second-generation designs can incorporate improvements based on experience with the original, the original will always be known as the first. The Houston Astrodome, although more expensive than subsequent encapsulated play areas, nevertheless has attracted millions of spectators, as well as millions of dollars worth of publicity. (See Fig. 3-2.)

Similarly, we now have very sophisticated air bubbles in pleasing shapes and designs, but the first-generation bubble, the prototype on which thousands of others were planned, appeared at the Forman School in Litchfield, Connecticut, in 1963 (Fig. 3-3). It was almost totally subsidized by the manufacturer and others interested in this new form of technology. The same can be said of the early users of synthetic surfaces, rooftops, and geodesic domes. Those who were first served themselves well: they got the facility they needed, plus many concomitant benefits. Newness in and of itself is not a reason for selecting any kind of facility, but neither should it be a deterrent to serious consideration of its merit.

Fig. 3-1. The Capital Centre in Landover, Maryland. (Photo courtesy John A. Shaver, architect.)

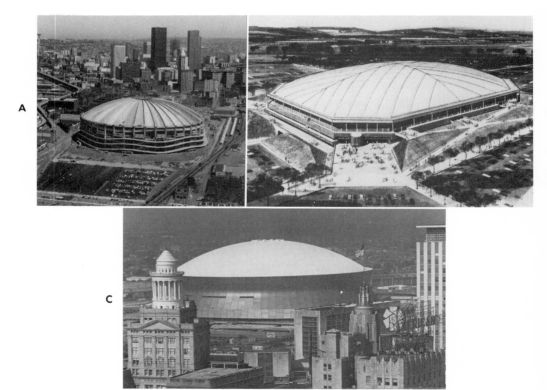

Fig. 3-2. A, The Kingdome is the King County Multipurpose Stadium in Seattle, Washington. **B,** Dome Stadium in Pontiac, Michigan, designed to house the Detroit Lions football team. (O'Dell, Hewlett & Luckenbach, Inc., architects.) **C,** The New Orleans domed stadium, larger than the Astrodome, depicts the new generation of super domes.

Fig. 3-3. Swimming pool and tennis courts under bubbles at the Forman School, Litchfield, Connecticut.

2. Flexibility versus permanence. It is no longer necessary to build for a hundred years or more. On the contrary, it may be desirable to build for a much shorter life expectancy and build a better facility as well.

In this country there are thousands of obsolete school buildings that are standing monuments to the solidity of their construction, but which have little or no value as places for learning in today's America. Suburban communities all over the country are now shrinking their school systems because the population that they served ten years ago has grown up and moved away. Many inner-city schools that once bustled with the excitement of neighborhood life are now surrounded by abandoned buildings, unused automotive garages, or other signs of urban decay.

Even if people still lived in these neighborhoods and had a school-age population to send to school, could these rigid boxlike fortresses of turn-of-the-century education accommodate today's classes with their openness, mobility, and technology? The answer is obviously no, and yet we still have a tendency to build unnecessary permanence into buildings, knowing all too well that educational methodology is anything but permanent.

In physical education this has been true to even a greater extent. We still build big basketball boxes that can optimally accommodate ten kids at a time. We still provide space-devouring bleachers in gyms that are used perhaps ten times a year. We still build traditionally, despite the fact that physical education programs point more and more to a different kind of facility. It is important to recognize that what is "hot" today will probably not be twenty-five years from now. Planning for flexibility becomes a key consideration in building for America's physical education facility needs.

We are not opting for tearing down everything that is old (Fig. 3-4). Landmarks and historical buildings should be protected. Every school building, however, does not fall into this category. We are certainly not suggesting that buildings should be temporary or of poor design or construction. Modern, suitable, and utilitarian buildings can be built without having to provide some

Fig. 3-4. The Yale University "Cathedral of Sweat", famed Payne Whitney Gymnasium, which opened in 1932, is a beautiful example of period architecture that houses many of the university's facilities and is still practical and functional. Within this structure, among other areas, are twenty-eight squash courts, eight handball courts, a basketball arena, two pools, golf practice areas, and accommodations for over 2200 spectators when necessary.

of the costly extras that skyrocket the cost of buildings. Interestingly enough, permanence is sometimes dictated by cost. When an unusually high cost factor is incorporated into a building, of necessity that building must have a long life. Financing costs for long-term buildings frequently add dramatically to the cost of the facility. All these factors must be examined in developing plans for building.

3. *Today's technology can build you anything.* "It can't be done" is no longer an acceptable answer to requests or suggestions presented for facilities. True, there are constraints placed on any building project imposed by budget considerations or perhaps zoning regulations, but beyond that today's construction technology can build almost anything. Arenas, field houses, and other sports facilities are housed in almost every conceivable space, with astounding design characteristics that overcome almost every conceivable restriction of the site. There are subterranean facilities, cantilevered facilities, and facilities split by running streams or busy interstate highways. In short, if an idea is valid and makes a contribution to the program, it must be advocated. What originally appears to be a major obstruction might turn out to be a successful innovation.

STEPS IN THE PLANNING PROCESS
Establishing the need

Reasons for wanting a new facility must be established. Does the tennis program suffer from lack of courts? Is there an obvious need for an ice skating rink that will attract families or groups?

Probably the most significant variable in establishing facilities, aside from cost, is the philosophy that shapes the form of each community's education. Is it a traditional system, or does it encourage experimentation? Are the schools run independently of other public agencies or is cooperation encouraged? Is the community able to pay for quality education? Is there general support for sports programs? All these, plus many others, tend to predetermine what can be expected for a facility or a program.

There are many steps; following are some of them.

Programs. Examine programs at communities that have similar education and recreational values and importantly, that have similar economic and social backgrounds. There is an interesting competitive aspect to the acquisition of new educational facilities. Sometimes the best rationale for a new facility is the fact that the neighboring community has one.

Current needs. Educational and recreational considerations must be fully examined before proceeding to generate support for a new building project. The educational and recreational needs of a community/school can be surveyed by questionnaires and by discussions with community activists.

Future needs. Perhaps a little more difficult is real understanding of demographic projections for the community. Will the population shift? Will there eventually be fewer young people and greater numbers of elderly in the community? Are there projections about transportation patterns? Will industrialization replace small commercial establishments in the community? Will the school/community be thriving in ten years, or will it be bereft of a clientele? These considerations, of course, are similarly part of the master plan projections, but it is wise to specifically identify the factors that will influence the proposed facility. Demographic projections can be formulated from federal and state sources (Census Bureau, Department of Transportation studies, federal financial aid statistics, etc.), as well as from local municipal studies. In a growing community the telephone company will have useful projections.

The master plan. The facility must be an integral part of the institutional master plan. Every public governing authority, except for the unsophisticated and perhaps the very small, has some sort of master plan for its development. The master plan is usually developed after lengthy involvement of the interested lay personnel and professionals of the community. The acknowledgment of physical education professionals that their needs are a part of the overall requirements of the master plan can immediately ensure the support of either the official or quasiofficial body charged with responsibilities of this nature.

Collateral forces

Probably the most time-consuming aspect of any major building or construction program is the fusing together of the many forces needed for a successful undertaking. In the final analysis, the letting of contracts is a step rather close to the termination of the project. It is the arduous and time-consuming intermediate steps between the germination of the idea and the first shovel of excavation that really separate the dreamers from the doers. Who and what are these collateral forces and how are they harnessed?

Professional staff. Teachers and coaches who will be working in the facility must be active supporters of the project. Not only is their professional expertise needed, but their personal contacts also provide a larger network for "spreading the word."

Clients. Those most affected by the facility will be students if it is a school facility, the public at large if a community recreation facility, and most probably both of these constituencies. They must be involved in the planning process, either individually or through organizations that represent them. Student government organizations and the local park and recreation society are just two examples of the multitude of affiliated groups who must be contacted.

Supporting agencies. The help of service and community agencies that have a stake in this new plan, such as the Parents' Association, Girl Scouts, YMCAs, service clubs, fraternal organizations, church organizations, and community betterment agencies, should be enlisted. Seek the support of respected spokesmen for as many of these groups as possible. They speak not only for themselves but also for their membership. Political clout leaves a bigger imprint when wielded by 10,000 citizens rather than ten. Organize these groups into a coordinated council to help the project.

Detractors. Touch all bases with those who see an adverse effect of the plan or who feel threatened by it. Meet with neighborhood residents and allay their fears about ruining a community. Be prepared to discuss any tax ramifications or potential changes in real estate zoning or assessment. People frequently want progress but not necessarily change. The rooted community interests are entitled to careful consideration, so take pains to see that they are informed and consulted about any new facilities that will have an impact on them.

In planning the middle school in East Orange, New Jersey, the school district used an effective technique. They took a five-month lease on an empty store on a main street adjacent to the school, where architects established a neighborhood design center. Here drawings and plans were displayed, community people dropped in to review them and to offer suggestions, and an unexpectedly sharp interest on the part of the local community contributed significantly to a fine facility. Their exposure to this aspect of the planning process generated much enthusiasm for the project. Once the school opened, the design center was no longer needed, and the store became an ice cream parlor.

Statewide or national professional organizations. Frequently, it is reassuring for local residents to hear of success stories in other parts of the country. Far-ranging professional organizations such as the American Alliance for Health, Physical Education and Recreation (AAHPER), National Recreation and Parks Association (NRPA), and National Education Association (NEA) can report on these successes, while at the same time lending their professional imprimatur to the project.

Political considerations. Politics not only means political governance but, in addition, the kinds of internal "planning" that keep institutions running. Who can best "push" the project? Is there a change of superintendents on the immediate horizon, and would the new official be more likely to favor the project than the incumbent? Is the new mayor or town councilman in need of immediate positive exposure in a particular community and would a new facility provide this? Perhaps the word "politics" conjures up a negative image in this context, and, if so, merely be reminded to take advantage of the every-day, internal organizational machinations that exist in every school system or community recreation department. This is neither unethical nor undesir-able. With so many valuable proposals vying for funding and approval from virtually every department of government or school, priority will be given to those able to garner the most support, both externally and internally.

The media. Make use of communications media to help generate support. The press, television, professional journals, and newsletters can be wonder-fully helpful. Sports news receives wide coverage in most American news-papers, and physical education and recreation personnel generally have good access to the sports pages of a newspaper. Look for opportunities to promote the new facility on these pages.

Once all the collateral forces have been identified and gathered together, the principle of cooperation should be established early in the process. The ad-ministration, architects, budget people, pupils, staff, and community represen-tatives must work closely to realize their goal. Therefore make certain that some vehicle is established early in the game that will bring these groups into regular communication. It can go by many names—a task force, committee, council, or consultative group—but whatever the name, the purpose is the same.

Special responsibilities of physical educators

An interesting and sometimes frightening paradox exists in the building of new facilities for physical education, sports, and recreation. In very few cases do school buildings or community projects emerge because they were con-ceived and promoted by high officials of government. Rather, they usually come about because of a groundswell or movement generated by one or two practicing professional physical educators who know little of architecture, fund-ing, or design. And rightly so. Although politicians, designers, construction specialists, and financial managers are all essential for converting facility dreams into building realities, the professional who envisions finer opportuni-ties for people is really the key.

Therefore it is essential at the very beginning of any physical education facility project that physical education teachers recognize how vital their role is.

Role of physical educators at the planning table. No one knows more about program needs than the professional physical educator, and no one can speak better from firsthand experience about the nitty-gritty problems of running a facility. This input is vital. It is the physical educator and fellow professionals who will be charged with the responsibility of running programs, supervising the locker rooms, moving equipment and people, and otherwise managing a facility. So solutions that appear to be feasible but in fact are not must not be permitted to be imposed on the professional staff. The physical educator can sit by quietly when load-bearing beams or amortization of bonds is discussed, but must speak up positively about such things as placement of gymnasium windows or types of gymnasium lockers. Perhaps the classic example of this admonition is a meeting in which final plans for a multi-million dollar gymnasium were being decided on by an "expert" group of administrators, planners, architects, and construction engineeers. The proposed centralized gymnasium complex was well facilitated to serve four schools that fed it. The locker rooms for all the teaching stations were fed by one corridor and two staircases, and all at the table agreed that the corridors and staircases were sufficient to serve the projected code requirements for 250 pupils per period. It was the beleagured, whistle-blowing "gym" teachers who reminded them that at the end of the period when 250 students leave the locker room, another 250 are entering, so the corridor and staircases would have to be able to handle 500 at one time, not 250. Only the "on the job" professionals spotted this, and probably every other teacher who had spent one day as a teacher in a gym would have recognized it as well. The building "experts," however, did not.

Limitations. Physical educators should not attempt to do things that other professionals such as the architect, budget director, landscape designer, purchasing agent, or legal representative can do better. In the same way that physical educators have been trained to know their jobs, the other professionals have been trained to do theirs. For example, as shown in Fig. 3-5, in building the facility at Millsaps College, a small, coeducational liberal arts college in Jackson, Mississippi, the architects, among their other services, developed materials that enabled the lay college community to visualize in advance what the eventual structure would look like and the purposes it would serve. So, instead of attempting to play a part for which they have not been trained, physical educators must monitor every step of the project so that the ultimate objective and concept of a fine facility will not be compromised. A good first step would be to "walk" through the plans with each constituency who will routinely use the building. Traffic patterns accessibility, maintenance, and other basic operational "hang-ups" will be easily identified in the process.

Professional standards. All local, state, and federal safety and health laws that apply must be planned for. Although these will be the responsibility of the construction professionals, physical educators should see to it that certain professional standards are met, standards that might not be known to others on the planning team. For example, the American Alliance for Health, Physical Education, and Recreation has recommended minimum standards for per pupil space allocations for new gymnasiums, and the Council for National Cooperation in Aquatics has developed minimum standards for pool decking. Physical

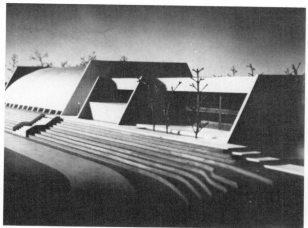
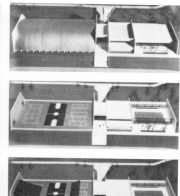

Project Millsaps College
Physical Education Center
Location Jackson, Mississippi
Architects Gassner/Nathan/
Browne
Consulting Engineers Ellers,
Reaves, Fanning & Oakley

Program To provide a multi-use facility for a private liberal arts college's program in physical education, intramural, and inter-collegiate competition, as well as an auditorium for campus and community use.
Design Solution To achieve the desired flexibility, the activity area is based on three 60' x 120' modules, each of which will accommodate one court

for either basketball, volleyball, tennis or 3 badminton courts. The center module can be used while the track is in use. The arched shape allows indoor tennis with minimum cubic feet of enclosure. Spectator seating for 2 - 3,000 is provided by telescoping and portable bleachers. Linear expansion of the building will provide for an indoor pool.

Construction and Materials
In the gym, aluminum standing-seam roof covers arched, laminated wood beams and decking. Various court layouts are taped or painted on the synthetic playing surface. Exterior walls are cast-in-place concrete with gray glass at openings.

Fig. 3-5. These renderings of the now completed facility at Millsaps College in Jackson, Mississippi, served as a ready frame of reference for interested parties during the planning and construction process. The accompanying text gives a brief and concise statement about some of the major construction considerations.

educators can make a major contribution to the planning process by familiarizing the architects with the names of the major professional organizations whose recommendations have generally become the standards of the professionals.

Physical education professionals would do well to arm themselves with a checklist as they prepare for the task of developing any new facilities. Checklists of this type can usually be obtained from any architectural firm that has had any experience in school building, professional organizations in the field, or professionals with expertise in this area.[1]

A FIELD GROWS IN BROOKLYN

The new Thomas Jefferson High School Stadium in Brooklyn (Fig. 3-6) is a graphic and dramatic example of the long and sometimes arduous process of creating a new facility for sports and recreation. In reviewing the "ladder" of events leading to the completion of the process, note that a minimum of one step was made on each rung of this ladder of succession, paralleling the steps described earlier in the chapter.

Something should be said of the location and history of Thomas Jefferson High School. The school stands like a beacon amidst a deteriorated and blighted

Fig. 3-6. Big Orange Stadium of Brooklyn's Thomas Jefferson High School. (Photo by Peter Ezersky.)

neighborhood in the Brownsville–East New York section of Brooklyn, one of the most volatile and depressed areas in New York City. Its athletic field, located two blocks from the school, was never of sufficient size on which to play but was used for physical education classes and practice for some varsity teams. As the area fell into disrepair, the field became horribly littered and a general sore spot among so many others in this crumbling community.

Concurrent with the most radical decline of the community and school was a remarkable record of success for its interscholastic football program, a source of much pride to an otherwise battered community. Jefferson players are sprinkled liberally throughout the ranks of college football powers with some making it big as pros, notably all-pro John Brockington. This football dynasty was molded on a glass-strewn, grass-bare, undersized practice field and through weekend visits to the fields of other schools.

Today's Thomas Jefferson multimillion dollar stadium can be directly attributed to the efforts of one man, Coach Moe Finkelstein, a dedicated professional educator whose planning procedures involved countless hundreds of hours of time and effort and similarly hundreds of people as the "collateral forces." The success of his efforts in spite of the numerous roadblocks along the way might serve an informational and motivational purpose for those who embark on similar projects.

In 1959, when Finkelstein took over as coach at Thomas Jefferson High School, he spearheaded a drive to do a feasibility study for enlarging their field.

The completed study showed the necessity of widening two streets to accommodate the field. Since one of the streets was a major thoroughfare, it became clear that this was an impossibility.

In 1960, Finkelstein formed what was to become the major force in the creation of the field: the Varsity Football Mothers' Club. Its first president was a dynamic organizer who immediately went after the political leaders, including the borough president, county and district Democratic leaders, and local representatives of the school board. Evidently this initial pressure paid off, and within three months there was agreement from the superintendent that Jefferson needed a field.

The next three years were spent in hunting for a suitable site. The one finally acquired after considerable frustration was located adjacent to a large landfill operation overlooking Jamaica Bay, a mile and a half from the school.

In 1967 the Division of School Planning of the Board of Education agreed to the site. In the same year Finkelstein and the other coaches and physical education staff developed a Bill of Requirements for the field. Their recommendations, among other things, called for separate fields for football and baseball. The Board of Education insisted on their usual requirements of a combination football and baseball field with a track superimposed around the field. Two years of heated negotiation with Board of Education representatives followed to get them to agree to the kind of field school personnel wanted. At the end of the second year agreement was reached that the new complex would contain a separate football and baseball field, an all-weather track, handball and tennis courts, an electric scoreboard, stands for spectators, and five rooms to be used for lockers and weight training.

Running concurrently with all these discussions was a continuous round of meetings involving parents, community leaders, faculty, political leaders, and student groups. Finkelstein has on file records of more than 200 separate meetings having to do with the eventual building of the field.

In 1967 the city administration pushed a master plan for redeveloping whole sections of the city, including the Jefferson field project. As a result of these abortive plans, construction was held up for three years. At the end of 1969 funds originally allocated for the project had been used elsewhere, and the field's proponents had to go through a whole series of complicated budget hearings to finally get the money rebudgeted.

In 1969, after ten years of fighting, not one shovelful of earth had been turned on the project.

Finkelstein acknowledges with gratitude the entrance into the picture at this juncture of a new president of the Varsity Football Mothers' Club whose knowledge and aggressiveness in making political contacts once again got the project rolling. She and Finkelstein orchestrated a whole series of meetings to overcome objections from some parents, local community leaders and Model Cities' officials who became fearful that a site one and a half miles from the school would in effect be a facility for the new residents contiguous to the field and not for the Thomas Jefferson High School community. The need for a united front was apparent, and once again the Mothers' Club president and coach had to cope with what had become an emotional and delicate matter. Two years passed, and, finally, building was started in 1971.

Finkelstein and other coaches became the literal on-site inspectors through every phase of construction. Even after the work started, delays and hassles cropped up. A three-month delay resulted because of a technicality in having the site transferred from the state to the city. There was constant conflict with Board of Education officials who had not had experience with this type of field. Four weeks before the field was completed the contractor still did not have authorization to use sod. Since the field was built on reclaimed beach land, and since traditional high school grass fields usually end up bald because of seeding, Finkelstein and his adherents demanded sod. They argued that since an expensive underground sprinkler system had been installed, it would be "penny-wise and pound foolish" to use seed rather than sod. This impasse at the eleventh hour was overcome in a manner typical to this project and probably typical to similar projects all over the country, that is, through a mix of community pressure groups, educational organizations, and civic leaders, who were able to get some direct political intervention. The $38,000 was finally approved for sod for the field.

In 1963 the original bid for the complex was $300,000. The 1971 bid was $1.2 million, the cost of the finished job.

The field opened in 1973; although there are still additional improvements to be made, the field is generally considered to be the finest high school football and sports stadium in New York City.

Finkelstein estimates that he spent an average of at least one evening a week working on the project for a period of fourteen years. Hundreds and hundreds of people were either directly or tangentially involved, and he freely admits to calling on every conceivable collateral force at his disposal in order to get the "Big Orange Stadium." Many professional experts in the field of sports facilities gave willingly of their time and effort.

Although a strong case can no doubt be made for the negative cost-economy of spending fourteen years on one project, there can also be little doubt that this stadium will serve thousands and thousands of city youth over a period of perhaps another fifty years. Contributions of this kind cannot be measured in traditional terms.

REFERENCE

1. Bronzan, Robert T.: New concepts in planning and funding athletic, physical education and recreation facilities, St. Paul, Minn., 1974, Phoenix Intermedia, Inc.

CHAPTER 4

Conventional buildings and building technology

Although it is generally easier to model a building or a building program after existing conventional designs, considerations of cost, technology, and program requirements mandate a full exploration of the options available to those in need of new sports facilities (Fig. 4-1). Any preconceptions about the best type of construction should be avoided until all avenues are fully explored. The full range of options available today is so diverse that a commitment to a single approach should occur only after probing investigation.

One approach, of course, is building a conventional brick, steel, glass, and mortar building. This conventional approach results in a conventional product, and the process through which this occurs is similarly conventional in nature.

The term *conventional* in no way denigrates this building technology. To the contrary, many facilities built in this manner are outstanding examples of aesthetically beautiful and functionally sound structures. For example, the magnificent new physical education center at the State University College at Cortland, New York, is built in a rather traditional manner and contains large gymnasiums, a competitive pool and ice rink, wrestling and gymnastics rooms, squash courts, corridors beautifully decorated with sports art, offices, and classrooms. It is big, attractive, and functional and serves the college and neighboring community well. When space and cost are not too limiting, a building of this type, well designed and planned, can house the best in physical education and sport facilities. Similarly, the Marriott Center at Brigham Young University in Provo, Utah, and Princeton's Jadwin Hall combine conventional building techniques with other somewhat less conventional approaches. (See Figs. 4-2 to 4-4.)

What are the mechanics of this approach? As you might expect, they are rather traditional. Artists' renderings and schematic drawings are prepared and reviewed by various committees composed of community representatives, the professional staff, construction specialists, etc. In essence, these schematic drawings provide a visual image of the thinking of the architects and physical educators. Details as to design and other technical matters are not included. Once the overall concept, site, and design are agreed on, exact specifications are prepared. These specifications, in addition to satisfying the aesthetic and functional requirements for the building, must also comply with existing building codes and regulations. This is a time-consuming process, and the physical education specialist can avoid extra charges by being on time and on target with the programs to be used in the structure.

Fig. 4-1. Six-building complex at the University of Utah connected by underground corridors and college health facilities.

Fig. 4-2. The Marriott Center at Brigham Young University in Provo, Utah, is a great place to watch basketball, but it is also the largest on-campus arena in the United States. For the past two years it has led the nation in average home game attendance, with 21,818 per game. This arena has a 23,000 capacity.

   Once all specifications are completely set down, the local procedures for bid letting must be followed. Final contracts are awarded, and construction begins. After this point any changes in program or building requirements in the classic building procedure become very expensive and often time consuming. The reason is obvious. The contractor is working within a given budget based on stated building specifications. Changes that occur after the contract is let result in increased costs. At the risk of redundancy it should be emphasized again that the specifications must be reviewed and understood before the contract is let.

   The remainder of this conventional building process is rather easily under-

Fig. 4-3. Jadwin Hall, Princeton University, combines innovative striking design with some traditional building technologies.

Fig. 4-4. The Assembly Hall of the University of Illinois, Champaign, Illinois. (Photo by Hedrich-Blessing.)

stood even by the layman. Various subcontractors come in to do the plumbing, electrical installation, carpentry, and masonry. The process is monitored along the way by the architect and prime contractor, and usually the key physical education professional in the community takes a rather personal and paternal interest in watching the "castle" rise. Many municipalities find it advisable to assign a full-time project manager or on-site engineer to ensure that the contractors are adhering completely to the specifications set forth in the plans.

The problems that usually accompany the traditional building process, as well as the traditional building product, are again well known. Any extension of time generally results in skyrocketing costs in labor and materials. Any particular industry-wide problem can adversely affect the completion of the building. For example, if plumbing materials or plumbers are not available on schedule, the whole project is delayed. In spite of these rather well-known problems, probably 90% of the building in this country is done in this fashion; reliable construction engineers, architects, and contractors working with interested professionals in education can and will continue to produce some outstanding facilities for physical education.

SYSTEMS CONSTRUCTION

Basically, systems construction means that buildings are built in a factory and assembled on site. The major building subsystems are predesigned and preengineered. Units are factory constructed and shipped to the site for installation. The layman usually refers to these buildings as prefabricated or modular buildings. These buildings offer a wide range of possibilities for exterior and interior design. In broader terms, a systems approach means that a problem is solved in an orderly process that begins with definition of goals, moves to analysis of how to achieve them, and finally proceeds to actual solution. Systems building was introduced in the United States in 1962, and, interestingly enough, schools were major clients. The one-level sprawling schools that dot so much of the American landscape are testimony to the systems approach. More sophisticated designs and technology now enable facilities to be built in this fashion while escaping this sameness of appearance.

The prolonged construction time of many projects renders buildings obsolete the day they are completed. A viable school building program therefore depends in large measure on effecting economies in both time and money. Systems construction has managed to control the length of building time and subsequently the costs of construction.

Ideally, systems building goes through four stages:

1. Study of user requirements
2. Establishment of performance standards for the building subsystems or the entire system
3. Integration of individual building subsystems into a coordinated building system
4. Testing of components (or subsystems) to assure that they satisfy performance standards

One begins, always, by describing the way in which a facility must work. Then portions of the project are isolated for open, competitive bidding, creating a series of solutions, or subsystems. It is a condition of each solution that it must integrate with all the others, a requirement that fosters cooperative efforts on the part of many subcontractors.

Since many components of the structure are finished inside a plant, the chance of delay caused by bad weather is minimized. Construction systems are erected quickly, enabling inside work to proceed uninterrupted by unfavorable weather. Site construction depends on a builder's ability to apply the modular systems to a particular type of structure. The full value in systems construction depends on the builder's performance in fitting the "jigsaw" pieces together.

Fast track scheduling

A relatively new management technique known as *fast track scheduling* provides crucial timesaving elements of systems building. Phases of a project, from design to construction, that normally follow one another in sequence can proceed in either parallel or overlapping fashion; therefore significant amounts of time can be saved. Fast tracking operates on the basis that any phase of a project can be begun on a foundation of generalized knowledge, with specific needs determined at a later date without any loss of efficiency in the design and construction processes. The systems approach permits design and documentation time to be reduced drastically. The few drawings necessary for the systems part of the project can be issued as soon as basic design decisions are reached. Thus fast track scheduling can be applied. Those parts of the building which take the longest time to construct, such as foundations, may be begun immediately.

Prefabricated buildings

Prefabricated buildings are ready-made structures that can be purchased in the same way one purchases a pair of shoes (Fig. 4-5). Components are aesthetically pleasing and can stand on their own in today's world of architectural design. They are flexible structures that can be surfaced with any known materials to achieve special effects or to emphasize a particular period theme. Restaurants and diners that are basically prefabricated, but whose facade and decor reflect different architectural periods, exist all over the country (Fig. 4-6).

Prefabrication is basically a systems construction technique devised to save money. Most manufacturers will generally offer a complete line of building styles and variations. The warehouse concept fits neatly into the recreation world. Prefab builders usually offer complete services from basic space design concepts through construction. Some sales organizations will provide moving-in services to the customer.

Fig. 4-5. Prefabricated structures at College of DuPage, Glen Ellyn, Illinois. (Photos courtesy College of DuPage.)

Fig. 4-6. Northern Oklahoma Junior College, Tonkawa, Oklahoma. Individualized fronts and entrances serve to customize preengineered buildings. (Photo courtesy Behlen Manufacturing Co., Columbus, Nebraska.)

Fig. 4-7. Exterior, **A,** and interior, **B,** views of gymnasium at the University of New Mexico, Albuquerque, New Mexico. (Photo courtesy Behlen Manufacturing Co.; Dick Kent, photographer.)

SITING

The siting of a facility often determines the type of construction that will be used; consequently builders and architects have substantial interest in site selection. Site examination will establish whether extensive landscaping and earth movement are required. It is difficult and expensive to build on severe slopes and in low-lying areas. Such sites may preclude the use of prefabricated structures and might also lengthen the construction time of a conventional structure. The University of New Mexico basketball pavilion is an excellent example of utilizing the terrain by doing site work with heavy equipment and pouring concrete seats on the earth (Fig. 4-7).

In planning gymnasiums or stadiums that will have large spectator capacities, proximity to well-developed highways must be considered. Traffic flow and accessibility during critical rush hours is as much a siting problem as is the slope and topography of terrain, particularly for the urban school.

MAINTENANCE FACTORS

Each type of structure has distinct advantages and disadvantages. However, in each case it is the school's responsibility for all repairs internally and externally. The cost of replacement of building materials and mechanical equipment varies according to the type of material and the amount of labor involved. Regardless of the grade of materials, the cost of labor is generally about the same. Initial economies envisioned by sacrificing quality materials are usually transient. In the long run maintenance and replacement costs may exceed the savings obtained with inferior or cheaper materials.

The skills of the school's maintenance staff must therefore be weighed against the cost of outside contractors. Costs of materials and of basic maintenance is a known factor in every community. A highly skilled staff is required to properly maintain automatic folding doors and mechanical bleachers, which are likely to become inoperative from time to time. Each type of construction requires different maintenance procedures as to skills and time. Careful studies must be made to determine which skills are or are not available. A minimal requirement of skilled labor is preferable because increasing salaries will continue to drive maintenance costs upward. The less time required for construction, the less interim financing will cost.

EXPANSION AND RENOVATION

If expansion, renovation, or possible contraction of space is anticipated in the future, the type of construction assumes even greater importance. It is particularly important if a program is likely to change. Community growth is difficult to anticipate, and physical education facilities should be designed to allow conversion to other uses if the need arises. Once a building has been completed, it is frequently impossible to correct the mistakes of inadequate planning, and it is costly, always costly. However, any additions or alterations should be less expensive, and the foresight built in originally generally more than offsets the larger initial expense. Without advance planning, future expansion will most certainly bring less space than the original construction dollars would have brought.

To benefit from design that anticipates future expansion, some flexibility should be provided for several alternate approaches. Therefore it is important not to get locked in with plans that are costly to change.

•   •   •

In summary, before choosing a particular type of building:

1. Carefully review all possible sites, considering soil condition, utility installation costs, zoning laws, building restrictions, traffic patterns, transportation facilities, access to outdoor fields, and student traffic patterns.

2. Plan a building that allows for flexibility of programs and can be easily expanded in the future.

3. Consider carefully the hidden factors such as what it will cost to heat and cool a facility. Allowance should be made for alternate energy sources.

4. Insist on maintenance projections for any type of building planned.

CHAPTER 5

New technologies in athletic surfacing

A casual observer of the sports and recreation scene in the United States can easily recognize not only the vast geographical differences that exist between New York and California, but the programmatic and participatory differences that exist as well. People play outdoors all year in California, usually on reasonably green fields in a reasonably comfortable climate. People play under similar circumstances in New York for only about three months a year, after which weather forces them inside to inadequate space and poor substitutes for outdoor programs.

About 1960, we, among others, began to expound the theory of providing physical education in the northern states like that found year round in California. The one variable, of course, that could not be controlled was the weather and its concomitant effects on grass. How did one get year-round play facilities in a natural climate like that found in the northeastern United States? The answer, of course, has become well known all over the United States. In a short period of about fifteen years there has been a radical change in the recreation habits of all Americans. Year-round tennis, swimming, ice hockey, and other sports are commonplace in every section of the country, regardless of natural climatic and geographical conditions. The two factors most responsible for this phenomenon are synthetic playing surfaces and lightweight, reasonably priced structures that enclose these playing surfaces.

Chapters 5 and 6 deal specifically with these two options in sports facilities.

Synthetic surfaces have proliferated throughout the world in the past several years. The most enthusiastic clients in terms of number and variety of installations have been educational institutions in the United States. The most elaborate facilities are found at Olympic Stadiums and stadiums used by professional sports teams. Originally, however, the product was designed to provide an all-purpose, all-weather surface for children.

Prior to the development of synthetic materials, a search for a perfect hybrid strain of natural grass that could survive under constant year-round usage proved unsuccessful. Physical educators had resigned themselves to "bald-headed fields." In 1957 interest in the development of synthetic playing surfaces was stimulated by the educational community, as well as by industry, which saw a vast commercial potential in recreation surfaces. In northern climates in the spring, baseball was not as much scheduled as it was postponed because of unplayable fields (Fig. 5-1). Athletic directors and coaches began to realize that mud was obsolete for football. Furthermore, according to Harold B. Gores, president of the Educational Facilities Laboratories, every child in America is entitled to an "acre of June" on which to play. Why couldn't American technology address itself to finding suitable year-round recreational surfaces? Was there something sacrosanct about playing on nature's soil, so often unsuitable for play? Was ground-level participation an essential factor, or was it conceivable to play on rooftops or in basements or in other heretofore unused places for play?

Fig. 5-1. Unplayable fields are becoming less of a problem for administrators and players.

Fig. 5-2. An all-synthetic stadium in Portland, Oregon.

This kind of thinking sired the proliferation of carpets designed to replace nature's fragile product (Fig. 5-2). Synthetic materials make possible playing surfaces that offer maximum benefits to all participants at economical cost. In addition, several concomitant benefits accompany their use. Studies indicate that the impact of falling is no greater than falling on the usual playground or sandlot field. If it is left uncovered, rain drains easily with the contour of the field. It serves as a cushion for anyone tumbling from a piece of playground or gymnastic equipment (Fig. 5-3). Most important, a ball striking the surface always responds with a uniform and predictable bounce. There are no "bad hops." For example, a baseball moving across a synthetic surface may move more rapidly but will behave in a more predictable manner. (See Fig. 5-4.)

Portability is an additional positive factor for major coliseums, mobile spectator promotional activities, and portable parks in blighted urban areas.

Synthetic surfaces display characteristics that are both different and similar to grass and traditional wooden gymnasium floors. The color and appearance of grass is desirable, so imitation carpets similar to a grass surface in color and complete with individual blades were introduced to the sports world (Fig. 5-5). The decline of the "bald field" was at hand, and children no longer had to look forward to playing in the mud at recess time.

A second type of surface, smooth or pebbled, was manufactured to replace gymnasium floors and dirt field house floors (Figs. 5-6 to 5-9). Surfaces capable of accommodating tennis, basketball, track, and games previously played on asphalt, cinder, cement, clay, or wooden surfaces are now available.

In the early stages of research and development the products manufactured

Fig. 5-3. Synthetic matting provides a safety cushion under playground equipment.

for field use were attempts to imitate nature's grass. Synthetic blades of grass were developed for these man-made surfaces. But what did the actual blade of grass on a synthetic surface accomplish? Natural grass becomes a lubricant when crushed underfoot, permitting slippage and helping to prevent the locking of the foot to the surface, which causes some leg injuries. Independent studies indicate that physical injuries can be reduced if the impact of the body

Fig. 5-4. Synthetic fields are now commonplace in professional baseball.

Fig. 5-5. Some golf greens feature artificial blades of grass.
(Photo by Carl Dixon Associates.)

Fig. 5-6. One of the first synthetic installations, the Moses Brown Fieldhouse,
Providence, Rhode Island. (Photo courtesy The Monsanto Corporation–Astroturf
Recreation Surfaces.)

Fig. 5-7. The Fieldhouse, University of Iowa, Iowa City, Iowa.

Fig. 5-8. University of Pennsylvania's Franklin Field.

Fig. 5-9. Synthetic indoor track at Wilton Senior High School, Wilton, Connecticut. (Photo by Bill Rothschild, Monsey, New York; courtesy Schofield & Colgan, Earl R. Flansburgh, Nyack, New York, architects.)

force directed to the playing surface can be partially diffused in two directions —down and to the side. Although synthetic blades of grass are aesthetically attractive on a field, they do not necessarily add to its playability. So synthetic surfaces that are smooth or pebbled but do not contain the "grass blades" were produced. However, to provide for this necessary slippage, most new installations now have added ingredients that address themselves to the problem.

Synthetic products for athletic recreation surfaces proved to be practical and economical because they offered a solution for greater surface use and much fuller utilization of fields.

School administrators then requested a surface on which they could set chairs and other school equipment. In addition, they specified that the removal of furniture should not leave the surface scarred or indented. In other words, the surface must be resilient and able to resume its original characteristics after each use. Most products now available have such a "memory." However, the "memory" varies from product to product, and the facility planners should insist on a guarantee of performance for this characteristic. Companies can vary the hardness of their products from very soft to extremely hard, and they can control the degree of "memory" and resiliency. (See Fig. 5-10.)

An equally significant positive factor in the "coming of age" of synthetic surfaces is that a field now may be placed "in the sky," affording new recreational surfaces where natural grass will not grow (Fig. 5-11). An additional positive appeal of synthetic fields is that they opened up participation in a wide range of recreational sports that were formerly limited by climatic factors.

Fig. 5-10. Graceland College Fieldhouse at Lamoni, Iowa, features a synthetic floor in a 300- by 175-foot cable structure with formboard/foam roof structure.

Fig. 5-11. Rooftop football atop the gymnasium building at Knoxville College, Knoxville, Tennessee. (Photo courtesy Gassner Nathan Browne, architects.)

55

Synthetic fields are suitable for other spectator attractions such as rock concerts, marching bands, student fairs, and exhibitions. With the advent of nationwide color television coverage of major sports events, the consistency of color afforded by synthetics has added considerably to the attractions of sports (Fig. 5-12). Additionally, the "carpet" aspects of certain synthetics provide for a mobility and flexibility heretofore unknown. Fields can literally be rolled out like carpets and then rolled up and removed after use. Tennis in densely populated inner-city streets can now be played on courts that literally can be rolled out and up and then transported to another street. (See Figs. 5-13 and 5-14.)

The fire hazard of synthetic products has been overstated. The materials will support combustion under extreme conditions, but most authorities agree that the chances of fire are negligible.

The one problem that does exist, more aesthetic than dangerous, is created by smokers who ignore caution signs and receptacles and throw their flaming cigarette butts on the synthetic surface. The burning cigarette butt leaves a small elliptical black mark on the surface. Unfortunately, it will not wash off. Although unsightly, it does not affect performance of the surface.

Maintenance is necessary on any of the surfaces. Any surface will collect dust, dirt, and debris that must be cleaned. Cleaning costs approximate those of traditional surfaces, but replacement and refinishing costs are practically eliminated.

Savings inherent in synthetic surfaces have been similarly overstated in

Fig. 5-12. Halftime spectacles covered by television look good on the colored surfaces of synthetic fields. (Photo courtesy 3M Co. and University of Wisconsin Sports News Service.)

Fig. 5-13. The University of Idaho's portable Tartan turf football field.

Fig. 5-14. Noonday tennis exhibition on portable Uniturf court at the Prudential Center in Boston, Massachusetts.

terms of maintenance and understated in terms of use. Maintenance costs of outdoor installation of synthetic grass are reduced because it does not need watering or mowing and will remain green. The original installation, however, is expensive. The concept of *cost per use* should be studied and compared to maintenance costs for natural turf. The actual count of the number of times a surface is used and the number of participants becomes important in the comparison of costs. For example, Boston University's synthetic grass field is used for varsity teams, intramurals, college recreation, and physical education classes. The field is lighted, and it is not unusual to see student intramurals at 11 P.M. Hofstra University uses its field for its intercollegiate teams but also to generate revenue: on one weekend there were nine separate football and soccer spectator games running from Friday afternoon through Sunday night, featuring high school through professional athletics.

SYNTHETIC GRASS SURFACES

A brief review of factors to be considered in installation of synthetic grass surfaces follows:

1. *Appearance.* An artificial turf with individual blades protruding from a resilient base makes an excellent surface for all field sports.

2. *Pile.* The materials are available in varying pile heights and thicknesses, depending on specified uses.

3. *Shoes.* Synthetic grass is not hard on shoes. Cleated shoes can be used. Molded multistudded soles or gym shoe soles seem to function best.

4. *Wear.* If the materials wear out, they can be patched. Original installations made in 1967 and 1968 are still in daily use. Intense heat will melt the fibers at the area of contact (e.g., burning cigarette marks).

5. *Installation.* It is recommended that the material be placed on a paving. There are many cases, however, in which the material has been placed directly on dirt.

6. *Permanency.* It is usually recommended that the materials be permanently adhered.

7. *Seams.* Seams can be sewn, taped, zippered, or welded.

8. *Lines.* Lines can be painted or chalked.

9. *Cleaning.* Material can be brushed, vacuumed, or washed.

10. *Weather.* The material is more slippery when wet. Moisture does not seem to affect the life of the product. However, it is recommended that water be vacuumed off prior to any contest. It can be used successfully indoors or outdoors.

11. *Color.* Intense sunlight over an extended period of time has caused material to change color very slightly. A check should be made with the manufacturer for color guarantee. All companies involved have made great strides in overcoming any color changes.

12. *Problems.* Problems have included heat, durameter (hardness), nap direction, seams, cleaning, burns, and injuries.

SMOOTH OR ROUGHED NONGRASS SYNTHETIC SURFACES

Basic qualities are as follows:

1. These synthetic materials can be soft or hard as specified by the company. This material makes an excellent durable all-purpose floor for smooth surface contests or other uses such as basketball, tennis, conventions, track, physical education classes, commencements, cocktail parties, or community gatherings. The "gym shoes only" signs may be discarded, and both cleated and flat shoes may be used.

2. These materials are not easily disfigured. A steel cleat or high heel will sometimes cause a small scratch. A small track cleat will mark a smooth surface but usually does not show a mark on the pebbled surface.

3. Seam problems apparent in early products have been reduced. The poured surfaces (bulk) seem to have fewer surface problems. The synthetic top surface usually will outlast the undersurface.

4. Installation recommendations are that materials be adhered to a solid subsurface. These materials can be patched. They will mar in the event of a fire, and a burning cigarette butt can leave a permanent mark. In some installations the surface does not have to be adhered to a permanent base and can be portable. In most instances, however, it is advisable to permanently adhere these materials to the surface beneath.

5. Weather and moisture do not adversely affect the products.

6. Lines can be molded in the product, taped, painted, or chalked.

7. Materials can be brushed, vacuumed, or washed by hand or machine.

8. Materials in use indicate an indefinite life span.

9. They seem to be nonallergenic.

10. Before making a decision, it is wise to visit such installations as the following:

> Gymnasiums
> Cages, clear-span
> Locker rooms and showers
> Tennis courts, portable and permanently installed
> Tracks, "440" outdoor, 8-lap indoor, and 11-lap indoor

11. Costs vary in proportion to the thickness of the material and type of synthetic. Most of these synthetic surfaces are basically urethanes, polyvinyl chlorides, or rubber.

12. Surface finishes may be purchased and applied to facilitate cleaning.

13. Recommended thicknesses are as follows:

Varsity basketball, university	3/8 to 1/2 inch
Tennis	3/16 inch
Recreation	1/4 inch
University track	3/8 inch

14. A small amount of slippage to a smooth-soled shoe seems desirable on these surfaces because it tends to reduce injuries to the lower leg.

CHAPTER 6

New technologies in structures

The use of new building technologies was a rather sequential follow-up to surfacing breakthroughs. As synthetic surfaces were perfected and placed inside buildings, on top of buildings (Fig. 6-1), on piers, and under bridges, it became quickly apparent that lightweight structures offered a plausible and economical solution to the problem of putting a building around a play surface. Fortuitously, these technologies were ready just at the time that women's athletics, among other factors, spurred the need for additional facilities. The boom in community center/school growth and the recreation explosion had rendered the familiar basketball box inadequate for the physical education and recreation needs of almost every community. Conventional building techniques often required four to seven years from planning to completion, so the 1960s provided the perfect climate for the tremendous boom in lightweight structures.

Pneumatic structures offered educational planners an exciting and dramatic alternative in new building technology (Fig. 6-2).

This technology responded to the necessity for "instant buildings which were needed yesterday." These portable, demountable, relocatable, inflatable, and pre-engineered structures became "hot items" in the sports facilities industry.

During the 1960s membrane structures were increasingly used in educational institutions for enveloping recreational areas. In the United States the competition for the construction dollar made these lightweight shelters particularly attractive. As the shelters became sophisticated and were accepted as alternatives to permanent structures, the economy of lightweight construction became even more attractive (Fig. 6-3).

Initially the shelters were developed for reasons other than economics. The total freedom and openess possible within the structure reflected the trends of society mentioned in previous chapters. Although the question of whether total encapsulation can produce a livable environment for man has not been fully determined, much valuable knowledge has been acquired about human habitability. The U.S. Pavilion at Osaka at the Japanese World's Fair (Fig. 6-4) and the burgeoning tennis centers (Fig. 6-5) all over the world bear testimony to the practicality and effectiveness of this kind of encapsulation for recreation structures and warehouse use. In the United States and Canada inexpensive indoor space has been obtained with membrane structures, much of it excellent recreation space. Savings in the cost of protective structures en-

Fig. 6-1. Gymnasium on the roof of New York Polytechnic Institute in Brooklyn, New York.

Fig. 6-2. Air structures add dramatically to the night sights.

able the owner to utilize more funds for space acquisition, providing greater space at less cost.

The familiar pneumatic structure, "the air shelter," or "the bubble," can be fabricated in virtually any size or shape (Fig. 6-6). However, they all operate on a very simple principle. Air is forced into a large baglike structure that can be shipped and stored as a small deflated package. It is anchored to the earth or surface on which it rests to avoid any great loss of pressure, and air is forced into the balloon in the same way a child's balloon is inflated. The entrance is generally through an air lock. The membrane may be reinforced by cables running over the top of the structure or laced to the underside of the membrane in order to reshape and stabilize the structure. Internal pressure is maintained

61

Fig. 6-3. Mercer Island Country Club, Seattle, Washington. (Photo courtesy Educational Facilities Laboratories, Inc.; Peter Green, photographer.)

Fig. 6-4. Entrance to United States Pavilion, 1970 World's Fair, Osaka, Japan. (Photo courtesy Japanese Tourist Organization.)

Fig. 6-5. Exterior, **A,** and interior, **B,** views of air-supported tennis structure. (Photo courtesy Air-Tech Industries, Inc.)

Fig. 6-6. Air structures are used to "mothball" naval vessels.

slightly higher than external pressure. This pressure differential is not notice-able to people or animals, and it is this pressure that inflates the membrane and makes a building out of it.

Another type of air structure uses a construction base composed of con-crete, earth, or similar base material that surrounds the structure and is in-tended to offer structural stability and afford a lower membrane profile. Based on this principle, Charles Wright Academy, a private school in Tacoma, Wash-ington, built a simple field house with enough floor space for two basketball and two badminton courts. There are no mezzanines or basements or any bal-conies. Everything is on the ground floor under a 220 by 140 foot air-supported roof, except the locker rooms, which are located in a concrete block building at one end of the field house. (See Fig. 6-7.)

Two air-supported fabric structures form the new focal point for student ac-tivities at the University of Santa Clara in California. They house spectator seating for athletic competition, locker and shower facilities, student activity areas, and dining facilities. Swimming pool facilities are encapsulated in a smaller fabric structure with a retractable roof. (See Figs. 6-8 to 6-10.)

Milligan College, a small, coeducational, church-oriented college in eastern Tennessee, solved its need for a physical education–recreation facility by erect-ing an attractive air-supported roof structure at about half the cost of a conven-tional building. This dramatic addition to the campus was set into the rolling hills, which required a minimum of excavation, and at the same time main-tained a low profile that fit comfortably and aesthetically into the campus com-plex. By using an earth berm, columns, and other architectural modifications to attach the compression ring to the roof, the fabric roof can hang without touch-ing the floor when it has no supporting air pressure, thereby adding a com-fortable safety factor.

This structure, enclosing 68,400 square feet, houses a main basketball court with 1400 spectator seats, a swimming pool, locker room, and two large open

Fig. 6-7. Exterior, **A,** and interior, **B,** views of Charles Wright Academy's field house, Tacoma, Washington. (Photo courtesy Educational Facilities Laboratories, Inc.)

Fig. 6-8. Two air-supported fabric structures will form the new focal point for student activities at the University of Santa Clara, Santa Clara, California. The main area will be approximately 60,000 square feet and will be encapsulated with a skin of fiberglass fabric coated with Teflon. It will house spectator seating for athletic competitions, locker and shower facilities, student activity areas, and dining facilities. Swimming pool facilities will be encapsulated in a smaller fabric structure with a retractable roof. (Photo courtesy Caudill Rowlett Scott, design architects; Albert A. Hoover & Associates, principal architects; and Geiger Berger Associates, consulting engineers.)

Fig. 6-9. The Thomas E. Leavey Activities Center, University of Santa Clara, Santa Clara, California. Interior view of berm construction and cable-membrane roof.

Fig. 6-10. The Thomas E. Leavey Activities Center is an excellent example of the sophisticated pneumatic structure using earth berms and cable-membrane roofs.

A

B

Fig. 6-11. Exterior, **A,** and interior, **B,** views of Milligan College's physical education, relaxation, and intercollegiate athletic facility.

floor areas for a number of recreational activities, as well as service areas, offices, and instruction rooms.[3]

Milligan's commitment to this new form of technology is consistent with an interesting phenomenon in educational facilities planning: often small, privately supported institutions, faced with specific facility needs, take the lead in completing new and seemingly daring building concepts (Fig. 6-11). The Forman School in Connecticut with its pioneering bubble-enclosed swimming pool, the Moses Brown School's field house in Rhode Island with its experimental synthetic playing surface, and, more recently, LaVerne College in California with its tentlike fabric roof (p. 77) are some other easily recognizable examples of this trend.

The air beam structure used frequently in military installations (Fig. 6-12) is finding more proponents each year. This air structure consists of beams or arches filled with air, which then support an enclosing membrane. Side openings are possible. In this instance the structure is a hybrid between the pneumatic structure and the tensile membrane structure.

After a dozen years of intensive use and evaluation of pneumatic structures, certain generalizations regarding them can be made. Since each structure may serve a different function and develop a character of its own, it is recommended that the advantages and disadvantages be weighed carefully.

Problems in pneumatic structures have arisen with regard to heat gain, heat loss, acoustics, life of fabric, aesthetics, and building codes, all of which were

Fig. 6-12. Air beams for military installations have applicability for sports facilities.

overcome. On the positive side, the price for a pure shelter is less expensive than that for a traditional rigid building, and people seem to enjoy playing in the structure. Repair and maintenance are economical. The structure can be mobile, and the early fears of vandalism seem to be unfounded.

In essence it seems that as a pure recreational structure, the air shelter rates high both as a concept and as a product.

For example, when a small area the size of a tennis court (120 by 60 feet) is covered, the tendency is to use the court space as in the past, but now it can be used 24 hours a day on a year-round basis.

For smaller structures, the combination of conventional building methods with a membrane roof designed to open and close appears to work well (Fig. 6-13). It appears that pneumatic structures perform best when there is a greater space to be covered and that greater economy accrues as the size increases.

As the size increases, concept difficulties seem to occur as people tend to expect the pneumatic structure to perform like a conventional building. It must be remembered that the air shelter represents reasonably new technology and should not be expected to perform identically to a conventional structure.[1]

History shows that new building technologies undergo a period in which they are made to appear and perform like buildings to which people are accustomed. Care should be taken not to perpetuate this practice, particularly with regard to air structures.

As larger spaces have been studied and covered, the membrane has become virtually a roof like that on existing field houses, gymnasiums, stadiums, and coliseums. In the transition from the pure tennis "bubble" to the sophisticated larger structure, the idea of encapsulating space per se is lost. Economies tend to disappear, and antiquated concepts are perpetuated in the new technology. Membrane technology does not just mean putting a fabric roof on a standard building, although there are excellent examples of aesthetic and utilitarian facilities now in existence such as the all-purpose coliseum at the University of Northern Iowa (Fig. 6-14).

The vastness of the warehouse concept, the flexibility, and the recreational freedom that can accompany pure space and volume is lost when pure air technology is mixed with conventional building techniques. In essence, air technology suggests that we now think in terms of acres rather than in square feet.

If you relate the pure space concept to most institutions, to places where people of all ages gather, you will find that spot of ground that attracts people and their spontaneous activities. This unofficial recreation-activity center is where the action is: touch football, broomball, frisbees, sunbathing, casual soccer, even studying.

There are no rest rooms, changing rooms, concessions, spectator facilities, or offices. These unofficial activity areas do not even have buildings. They are merely places where people congregate.

Unfortunately, the climate can and does render these areas useless most of

Fig. 6-13. Cuyahoga Falls Natatorium in Ohio, a combination of a conventional building with an air shelter roof that provides for open air and enclosed swimming.

Fig. 6-13, cont'd. For legend see opposite page.

Fig. 6-14. Rendering of all-purpose coliseum for the University of Northern Iowa. This facility would include spectator seating for as many as 20,000, plus a full complement of physical education support facilities. (Courtesy Owens-Corning Fiberglass Corp.; Geiger Berger Associates; and Thorson Brom Broshar Snyder, architects.)

the academic year. Thanks to the encapsulation concept, however, these areas can be covered and uncovered as desired, affording everyone "an acre of June" at all times.

When the facility is covered, participants or nonparticipants should be able to use it in the same way they used it before. The wise builder will encapsulate the area in the simplest manner, allowing the air shelter to do what it can do best—encapsulate.

In a large structure the membrane is placed high above the head of the participants. A new environment is created, and no services are needed other than shelter.

When auxiliary items are added, several things occur. The program within the facility assumes a rigidity and a structured formality associated with school programs. Supervision becomes uppermost in the minds of the administrators. Money becomes a factor, and the facility is closed a great deal of the time. Vandalism tends to increase as the spontaneity of use decreases.

The fabric shelter as we know it today works well as an environmental cover placed over existing recreation-leisure areas. Because of the heat gain, which seems to present a more severe problem than heat loss, the northern areas of the United States seem to be better suited for environmental covers. They have many fields behind schools that can be entirely covered.

After the field has been encapsulated and made available for recreation, a secondary problem arises. Since nature's products cannot take the abuse of human feet all day every day, it usually becomes necessary to install a synthetic surface so that fullest utilization of the new facility is possible.

The small school district interested in encapsulating a football field for school and community must realize that the cost of even an unsophisticated

Fig. 6-15. Detroit Lions Stadium, Pontiac, Michigan.

structure will be high, but the total cost, including site work, lights, air mechanicals, surface costs, and entrances, will be less expensive than a rigid structure. In terms of economy, the cost per user cannot be approached by any other type of building structure.

On a grander scale, the 80,000-seat Detroit Lions football stadium (Fig. 6-15) in Pontiac, Michigan, has a fabric structure roof that covers ten acres, making it one of the largest fabric-enclosed areas in existence.

ADVANTAGES AND DISADVANTAGES OF AIR SHELTER TECHNOLOGY

An article in *Canadian Architecture*[2] listed the following advantages of air shelter technology:

1. *Low initial cost.* Air shelters allow a client with a small capital budget to acquire a facility that could not be obtained if conventional construction techniques were employed.

2. *Speed of erection.* The actual erection of the envelope takes only one or two days. However, additional time is required for the ground work, site services, foundation, anchorage, flooring, and installation of mechanical and electrical equipment. Only minimal field labor is needed.

3. *Ease of deflation, inflation, and repair.* Deflation and inflation of the fabric envelope do not require skilled labor. Many existing structures come supplied with repair kits. (The repair of a major fault requires skill and special equipment such as that needed for electronic fabric welding.)

4. *Portability.* When deflated and packed, the fabric envelope can be stored in a small space or easily transported elsewhere for storage or use. Depending on the size of the envelope, deflation and packing requires one or two days.

5. *Adaptability for temporary functions.* For temporary use, the air-supported structure has definite physical and financial advantages over a conventional building. A number of manufacturers are now preparing to lease their air-supported structures, which will increase their attractiveness for short-term use.

6. *Long-span and high-ceiling features.* Clear and unobstructed space is an inherent feature of the structure. Conventional long-span and high-ceiling structures are much more expensive. When the intended function demands these structural attributes, the air-supported structure may have a definite economic advantage.

7. *Integrated heating, ventilation, and air-pressure system.* The integrated system is also an inherent principle. Lengthy duct works and pipe works are not required. The warm-up time of the space is a matter of minutes.

8. *Maximum utilization of daylight illumination.* Translucency is a characteristic of some kinds of envelope fabrics. Artificial lighting is minimized during daytime use.

Disadvantages are as follows:

1. *Limited portability in certain applications.* The degree of portability depends on the type of construction (concrete foundations, conventional flooring such as wood), and site services such as gas and electricity are not portable.

2. *Life span.* The fabric envelope in use today has a life expectancy of up to twenty-five years, with longer-life materials being tested. All other items such as the foundation, flooring, and mechanical equipment have the life span of a conventional building.

3. *Poor thermal insulation.* The cost of heating is a significant factor and should be evaluated against that for a conventional building over time. During winter months when the heat is required to melt the snow or to cause it to slide off, a safe level of tem-

perature will have to be maintained at all times at the expense of heating costs. If the bubble is not to be heated during the inactive hours, it will have to be supervised constantly for the dangers of unexpected snowfall. In the summertime the heat gain of the air-supported structure poses a cooling problem.

4. *Acoustic problem.* The curved shape of the air-supported structure produces a peculiar acoustic environment. This poses limitations on its use for large gatherings and open-plan arrangements for different groups.

5. *Pressure.* Although the air pressure in the structure is only one inch of water column, some sensitive people feel a slight effect on their eardrums, particularly at the moment of entering the structure.

6. *Uncertain performance over long-term period.* Although the structure has undergone numerous tests by recognized laboratories, many long-term predictions are extrapolated from short-time tests. Some regard this kind of "accelerated test" as of little use, whereas others place great faith in it. Because of the short history of this type of structure, it is not yet possible to demonstrate performance value over time.

7. *Restriction due to wind.* In winds of hurricane velocity, most codes require that the structure be evacuated.*

TENSILE STRUCTURES

If climate, building codes, or community opposition militates against an air-supported structure, the tensile structure becomes a viable possibility. The tensile cable structure is not new to architecture. It is only new in terms of lightweight structures.

Most people will recognize the concept of a tensile structure by visualizing a traditional boy scout tent. It is a fabric supported by rigid columns. Supporting or restraining cables are carried directly to the ground anchor points and over poles or masts at stabilization points. Thus these lightweight structures do not require the considerable amount of construction materials needed in conventional buildings. The fabric, like that used on the air structure with cable-restraining nets, is noncombustible, self-cleaning, and maintenance free. The tensile structure can be partially opened (Fig. 6-16) when desired without affecting the stability of the building itself. It is as if the sides of a tent were rolled up.[5]

Where intense heat is a problem and air conditioning is too expensive, total encapsulation may only occasionally be desirable. Portability and mobility may

*From Canadian Architecture, pp. 12-13, Oct., 1972.

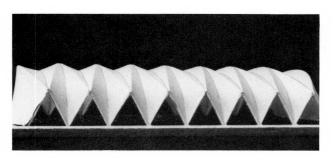

Fig. 6-16. Model of partially opened tensile structure.

be more advantageous. The aforementioned concepts offer an acceptable, even excellent, solution to the problem.

Although heat gain and humidity can be a problem in a pneumatic structure in a very warm climate, the tensile membrane structure affords an attractive alternative as a controlled physical recreation shelter. This kind of shelter lends itself easily to (1) preengineering, (2) capability of being erected quickly, (3) effecting the cost savings inherent in an air shelter, (4) relocation or demount-

Continued.

Fig. 6-17. The 1972 Olympic Stadium in Munich, Germany. (Photos courtesy German Information Center.)

Fig. 6-17, cont'd. For legend see p. 75.

ing, if desired, and (5) providing the alternate benefit of a totally closed building, or an open shelter as the situation requires.

The 1972 Olympic Stadium in Munich (Fig. 6-17) is an example of a sophisticated tensile membrane structure. LaVerne College, in LaVerne, California, was the first college in the United States with this permanent tentlike structure, a structure that houses a wide range of activities under its various dramatic roofs (Fig. 6-18). This small, coeducational college with a number of innovative programs was faced with the rather typical problems of space, cost, programmatic needs, and time. The college's response was to develop a building in which physical recreation, art, health services, and a student social center are all in one building with no doors separating activities, but in which each department's territory is clearly defined by the design of the structure. The building is square shaped, with semicircular segments along each side of it. The basketball arena is on a mezzanine, with offices underneath it. Each of the four segments houses different activities, such as an art studio, a gymnastics and conditioning area, a student health services unit, and a table game recreation area.

The LaVerne design and building technology lends itself easily to the wide variety of activities that must be accommodated in this college community. It also fits in easily with the openness, climate, and geography generally associated with this area of California.

The absence of support systems necessary for the most common type of air shelters and the elimination of air locks for entrances enable the entire structure to be opened at the sides, thus providing an area with a protective roof covering that is totally open and column free. One of the best examples of this can be found in the Gulf Breeze Community Schools Foundation Study.

Continued.

Fig. 6-18. LaVerne College, LaVerne, California. (Photos courtesy Educational Facilities Laboratories, Inc.; Peter Green, photographer.)

Fig. 6-18, cont'd. For legend see p. 77.

This planned educational community recreation facility (Fig. 6-19) has a central core of conventional type construction with two wings of demountable lightweight construction that provide an indoor/outdoor aquatic center on one side and a large clear-span gymnasium/field house/recreational center on the other.

This larger wing can be closed and heated in the winter, can accommodate crowds of 3500 for basketball, or can be kept entirely open for the community on all the beautiful days prevalent in a warm climate. This kind of permanent,

Fig. 6-19. Model of Gulf Breeze Community Recreational Facility, Florida. (Photo courtesy The Shaver Partnership; Walt Bukva, photographer.)

lightweight structure similarly provides for great economies in construction cost and time.

GEODESIC DOMES

The geodesic dome concept of construction, originally developed by futurist-philosopher R. Buckminster Fuller, has spawned some exceptional facilities for physical education and sport (Figs. 6-20 and 6-21). Because geodesic technology literally "builds upon itself," the end result is large open spaces with no pillars, posts, or supporting columns. The advantage for sports and athletic competition is obvious.

Perhaps the most striking example of this kind of facility is the J. Ralph Murray Athletic-Education Center at Elmira College in the Finger Lakes region of New York State (Fig. 6-22). This complex of three six-sided domes (and an adjacent natatorium) has provided a tremendous boost to the programmatic needs of this medium-sized, coeducational college. The gymnasium dome, a two-level affair situated between the other two domes, houses basketball, squash, volleyball, badminton, gymnastics, fencing, boxing, wrestling, and tennis. The field house dome accommodates all the traditional activities commonly found in large college field houses. The third dome is devoted to ice facilities, with a 191- by 85-foot rink and all the supporting services necessary for a full program of ice sports.[4]

79

Fig. 6-20. Geodesic dome, William Woods College, Fulton, Missouri.

Fig. 6-21. Geodesic membrane structure covering a swimming pool in Hicksville, New York. (Photo courtesy Dome East Corp.)

Fig. 6-22. A, World's first triple geodesic dome complex rises among rolling, wooded hills in Finger Lakes region of upstate New York. Three 232-foot TEMCOR domes house Elmira College's new $5.3 million Athletic-Education Center composed of field house, gymnasium, and hockey rink. **B** and **C,** The center TEMCOR geodesic dome, with its full-size basketball court and 2000 bleacher seats, offers excellent interior acoustics for concerts and convocations, as well as sporting events.

In addition to the functional aspect of this complex, its dramatic architecture has drawn considerable interest in and enthusiasm for the Elmira campus.

REFERENCES

1. A re-evaluation of air shelters, Scholastic Coach, p. 9+, Jan., 1974.
2. Canadian Architecture, pp. 12-13, Oct., 1972.
3. Educational Facilities Laboratories: Four fabric structures, New York, July, 1975.
4. The Elmira story, Scholastic Coach, p. 20, Jan., 1975.
5. Theibert, P. Richard: Coming on and going up fast, Scholastic Coach, p. 15+, Jan., 1974.

CHAPTER 7

Inside the gymnasium building

Although the exterior shell of any physical education building, be it a gymnasium or a specialized sports facility, can be looked on as a reflection of the work of the architects and other professionals in the construction industry, the interior can justifiably be a reflection of the skill and expertise of the physical education professionals. Although physical educators, of necessity, must leave considerations of design, stress, building codes, and structural materials to those who build buildings, the responsibility for what happens inside this building shell must fall directly on those who design programs—the professional physical educators.

The educator/user plays an important advisory and consultative role in all steps of the designing and building process; however, this role is much more critical and much more a leadership role when it comes to deciding what should happen inside the structure. The use to which a gymnasium building will be put depends almost exclusively on the programmatic functions that are assigned to it by the users. A community or school administration or physical education department that places heavy emphasis on basketball and places basketball as a first priority in program will have an interior gymnasium reflective of this interest—a basketball-"oriented" building. Similarly, if wrestling and weight training are heavily supported and "pushed" by the community/school, the interior trappings of any gymnasium will be planned to accommodate this interest. If the planning process for the building is approached intelligently, the proposed program emphasis should be reflected in this shell.

It becomes quickly apparent, then, that in planning the interior spaces, utilization projections must be analyzed carefully to allocate appropriate space for specific programs. In essence, each interior must be "personalized" to the program needs of those who will be using the facility.

For this reason, it would be impractical and probably counterproductive to go into detail about every interior facility possibility, since the user may have no interest whatsoever in half these possibilities. Rather, it is our intention to touch briefly on most of the possibilities for interior facilities, indicating the major considerations for construction, leaving it to physical educators to "custom" design the facility to their specific needs. These specific needs must be fully considered, since they bear heavily on the finished product.

Among the many questions to be asked are the following:

1. Will the gymnasium serve the entire program, required classes, and varsity sports?

2. If it is a college or university, is there a teacher education component and will service courses be accommodated?

3. Are there plans for a big spectator program requiring fees, public rooms, press facilities, etc.?

4. Will there be auxiliary facilities, or are they all contained in this one building?

5. Will there be extensive community use of the building?

6. If the facility is on a college campus, will it be available for the total college community, including faculty families, service personnel, etc.?

7. Will the building operate day and night?

8. Will the building house an academic core? Research facilities? Library? Considerable attention must be given to accommodating the academic program within the physical education complex.

9. Have enrollment projections been carefully studied so as not to overbuild and, similarly, to plan for expansion if necessary?

10. Is there one area that you want to be the center of student activity? If so, traffic patterns can be developed to bring students easily to this area.

11. Is interior design in concert with exterior landscape and design? For example, a heavily used lounge inside the gymnasium building should be accessible through attractive and well-planned outside areas, rather than through the "back door to the kitchen."

12. Are there other large open spaces on the campus or in the school to accommodate large crowds?

Measurements of courts, details as to ceiling heights, square footage requirements per pupil, and teaching station requirements are available from many sources, such as the American Alliance for Health, Physical Education and Recreation (AAHPER), the National Association of College Directors of Athletics (NACDA), and The Athletic Institute.[3,4] These basic factors must be clearly understood by physical educators before consideration is given to features of gymnasium interiors discussed in the remainder of this chapter.

EQUAL FACILITIES FOR BOTH SEXES

The advent of the famous Title IX of the Education Act Amendments of 1972, which mandates equal educational facilities for men and women, has stimulated some provocative thoughts on building athletic facilities. Women's sports activities are on a decided upswing. Not only are women competing on an interscholastic and an intercollegiate basis in women's sports programs, but they also compete alongside men in several sports. For this reason, it is essential that a rethinking of certain traditional concepts take place.

For one thing, there is no longer any justification for a "boys' gym" or a "girls' gym." All facilities should be designed for the use of both sexes. Even the training rooms, locker rooms, and figure control rooms should be planned for both sexes. It is no longer necessary to build separate and duplicate facilities. In some cases facilities can be used simultaneously, such as gyms, weight control rooms, and dance studios, whereas at other times, when propriety dictates, they can be programmed for single-sex use, such as locker rooms.

It may be necessary to design interior space so that a women's varsity game can take place simultaneously with a men's varsity game. No longer will women be expected to or be willing to defer their program while the whole gym is "opened up" for the men's varsity basketball game.

The necessity of providing accommodations for women's programs has mandated cooperative program planning between men and women. Title IX came along as a rather practical solution because the economics of building "separate but equal facilities" are such today as to preclude this as a viable approach. Rather, Title IX suggests a sharing of costs, space, and equipment, coupled with innovative and openhanded scheduling. It also dictates the elimination of labels so that the "boys' gym" or the "girls' pool" become "people places" instead. Indeed, some of the traditional barriers that existed between administrators, teachers, coaches, and students in sports programs may, of necessity, be coming down because of this legislation.

THE GYMNASIUM

The gymnasium is the space that usually serves as the basketball court or courts and is generally referred to as the main gym or court. These spaces can be divided by manually operated or electrically operated folding doors, so that

Fig. 7-1. Nets separate play areas in the gymnasium at Widener College, Chester, Pennsylvania. (Photo courtesy Behlen Manufacturing Co.)

the one large area can be divided into two or four or more separate stations. Gyms can also be divided by nets (Fig. 7-1), opaque curtains, movable self-supporting space dividers, or simply by placing gym equipment in such a way as to make natural barriers.

Usually, the "main" basketball court, the one that accommodates varsity games, is placed in the center of the gym so that as much spectator area can be opened as possible. Glass backboards are desirable on this spectator court for obvious reasons of visibility. Keep in mind that folding doors need places to fold up into and down to permit easy access to the open space. Keep in mind the acoustical ramifications of the various separating techniques, as well as the visual barriers that different kinds of dividers provide. Remember, too, that a gym divider can provide a clear, usable wall, which should be placed to optimize its utilization.

Since the main gym is frequently the site of a dance, concert, meeting, or other public event, the floor surface must be carefully considered. What is best for basketball might not be best for heavy use by a street-shoe crowd. Cost of maintenance, durability, initial installation cost, aesthetic and acoustical factors, speed of conversion, and resistance to cigarette butt marring are some of the many factors to consider. Combinations of surfaces are found rather commonly in newer gymnasiums. The options are many, and planning should in-

Fig. 7-2. St. Joseph's Academy. (Photo courtesy Caudill Rowlett Scott, architects; Roland Chatham, photographer.)

volve careful analysis of the positive and negative features of each surfacing material. (See Fig. 7-2.)

Storage facilities for the gymnasium have always been a source of problems. The myriad of equipment used in a typical program, coupled with the frequently heavy and cumbersome nature of much of this equipment, demands easily accessible and adequate storage. In addition to mats and gymnastics equipment and the usual assortment of balls, do not overlook the storage facilities required by the maintenance staff, food service people, ticket sellers and press, the varsity and intramural program, etc. In addition, if there is to be community use of the gym, remember that this group, too, has storage requirements. Place storage rooms where they are accessible and vandal proof. Make sure that shelves are provided and doorway openings are wide and high enough to accommodate the equipment. Provide for flush thresholds to storage areas, so that rolling equipment will not be hindered. Make provision for storage of "educational paper" essential to the program such as texts, charts, and evaluation instruments.

Special storage areas should be provided for expensive technical and scientific equipment such as movie projectors, videotape machines, jogging and respiration machines, and phonographs.

A desirable way to ensure adequate storage is to develop the specific storage needs of all who will use and service the gym, such as pupils, coaches, teachers, community, and maintenance staff, and then incorporate their requirements into the gym.

GYMNASTICS

Gymnastics activities can be accommodated in several ways. A common practice is to move the necessary equipment and apparatus such as mats, parallel bars, and vaulting horses into the main gymnasium, where instruc-

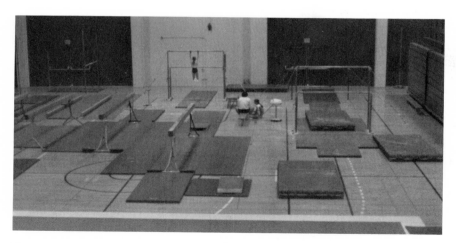

Fig. 7-3. Regular gymnasium setup to accommodate gymnastics.

tion or competition then takes place (Fig. 7-3). This arrangement requires careful consideration of wallboard and floor plate placement, as well as careful planning for seating approaches and safety. It usually requires considerable movement of apparatus to set up and dismantle frequently and speedily. The major objection to this arrangement is the inordinate amount of time wasted in preparing the area. Gymnastics equipment is large and cumbersome, and in many cases at least one third of the instructional time is spent on getting the area ready. Similarly, another objection is the wear and tear that the equipment is subjected to. Floors are scraped, mats are torn, and casters are broken rather regularly in this constant movement of equipment. The resulting "out of commission" equipment is a deterrent to any program, no matter how ambitious. Moreover, the custodial work required is usually abhorrent to students and teachers, who therefore look for ways to avoid the gymnastics unit. This approach makes it very inconvenient for students to participate in gymnastics because the preparation takes so long, particularly when measured against the ease with which basketball can be played, for example.

A more desirable approach to accommodating the gymnastics program is to provide a permanent area for this purpose where matting and other protective devices are permanently installed, where the equipment and apparatus is

Fig. 7-4. Women's Gymnastic Center, State University of New York (SUNY), Cortland, New York.

readily available and does not require constant moving (Fig. 7-4). In essence, students or other participants are taken to the equipment, rather than having to bring the equipment to the users. A tremendous savings in time and wear and tear is the result. This permanent gymnastics area can be equipped with adequate storage areas, training devices such as ceiling-supported harnesses, an audiovisual instructional area, and other supportive materials. If bleachers are added to accommodate spectators, then access areas, public toilet facilities, and other spectator factors must be considered.

Still another desirable method of handling the gymnastics program is a combination of the two approaches just described—building a relatively small and unsophisticated permanent gymnastics area for teaching and practice and moving other required equipment out into the main gym for competitions in which spectators are to be accommodated. In this way, except during the time when there is a varsity match, the large gym can be used for any number of other activities, and the gymnastics program can be running concurrently in the designated gymnastics gym.

In any case, certain basic factors should be kept in mind. Adequate space is required, more or less depending on the population to be served. The free exercise activities require a 42- by 42-foot mat, for which clear space has to be provided. Trampoline and horizontal bar activities mandate a minimum ceiling height of 24 feet. With running approaches and the need to keep participants from interfering with one another, it is suggested that an area of approximately 10,000 square feet be allocated for this activity.

Considering the stress and strain put on the apparatus when it is used, construction of this area should be planned with particular care, with ceiling beams capable of supporting ropes and other weight-bearing apparatus, with floor plates embedded in solidly constructed inserts, and with walls that will provide ample support for horizontal bars and similar gymnastics equipment. Doorways should have flush threshholds and be wide enough and high enough to handle the apparatus. Windows and lights should be placed so as not to present either a visual or physical hazard.

WRESTLING AND COMBATIVE ACTIVITIES

The popularity of competitive wrestling and various forms of martial arts that swept America in the late 1960s and early 1970s focused on the need to provide adequate facilities to accommodate these activities. Where at one time wrestling was rather exclusively limited to a small group of devotees, it is fast becoming a particularly popular spectator sport encouraging many more participants. In the past youngsters were only occasionally interested in the "manly art of boxing"; now there is tremendous interest in judo, karate, kung fu, and other techniques of self-defense. For a long while commercial enterprises took up the slack where public educational institutions failed to provide for these activities; but now more and more schools have added combative activities to their programs (Fig. 7-5).

Fig. 7-5. Combative Center, University of Utah, Salt Lake City, Utah.

The facilities and equipment needed for wrestling and combative sports can usually be shared, since the essential requirement is safe and resilient floors and walls. Most reputable gymnastics equipment manufacturers now produce polyurethane or other synthetic mats that are lightweight, durable, and safe. The surface on which these mats are placed should not be abrasive, since movement of the mats on the surface can result in tears and scratches. In situations in which traffic flow can be controlled and only properly attired participants can enter, it is desirable to have the floor permanently inlaid with this mat material, so that no time is required to place mats in position or remove them. In most situations, however, an undersurface of wood, plastic, or rubberlike material supports the mats that are positioned on the floor.

The wrestling mat should be 40 by 40 feet, so multiples of this basic size should be planned, depending on the size of the anticipated program. A 40- by 80-foot room will provide for two mats but will not provide for outside "walk around" space for those wearing street shoes. If mats are to be stored by rolling them up, remember that storage space will diminish any floor dimension by about 5 feet. Because of the aggressive nature of the activities accommodated in the wrestling room, the walls of the room should be of a similar resilient and padded material up to a height of 6 feet. Ceiling height should be at least 12 feet. The room itself should be free of any obstructions and protrusions such as doorknobs, wall-mounted supports, or bleacher appurtenances. The temperature of this room should be individually regulated. For competitive wrestling or combative activities, it is best to bring the necessary mats out into the main spectator arena, where fans, officials, and team members can easily be accommodated. This main spectator arena should be located at the same level as the combative room because moving wrestling mats to different floor levels is a difficult and time-consuming job. Elevators are generally not large enough to accommodate wrestling mats.

WEIGHT TRAINING, EXERCISE, AND FIGURE CONTROL ROOMS

No other activity in sports and physical education has enjoyed the phenomenal growth that weight training and figure control classes have. Where once "weights" conjured up the image of laborious and dull activity undertaken by a group of "muscle-bound" weight lifters, today the image is a positive one with appeal for participants, both men and women, in virtually every athletic endeavor. Weight training and exercise rooms can easily be shared by the sexes, and many universities report more use by women than by men. Weight training rooms can be used as classrooms, as part of any regular physical education program, or they can be used individually for recreational purposes. Most varsity athletes now have prescribed exercises to help in their preparation for their particular sport, and most individually prescribed physical fitness programs make use of the equipment found in these rooms. Although originally weight training rooms and equipment were the exclusive property of professional sports teams and well-financed universities, they are now rather standard equipment in many high school gyms, as well as in community recreation programs.

The impetus for weight training programs was provided when manufacturers produced rather compact, multistation pieces of equipment that accommodated upward of fifteen persons at a time (Fig. 7-6). Therefore, in planning for a weight training room, sufficient area should be provided to accommodate one, two, or more of these machines, depending on program needs. A mini-

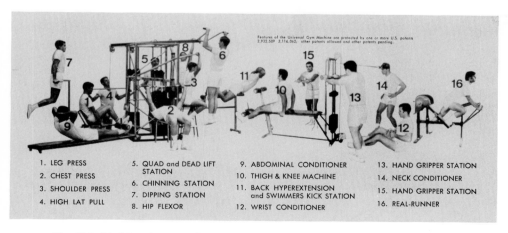

1. LEG PRESS
2. CHEST PRESS
3. SHOULDER PRESS
4. HIGH LAT PULL
5. QUAD and DEAD LIFT STATION
6. CHINNING STATION
7. DIPPING STATION
8. HIP FLEXOR
9. ABDOMINAL CONDITIONER
10. THIGH & KNEE MACHINE
11. BACK HYPEREXTENSION and SWIMMERS KICK STATION
12. WRIST CONDITIONER
13. HAND GRIPPER STATION
14. NECK CONDITIONER
15. HAND GRIPPER STATION
16. REAL-RUNNER

Fig. 7-6. Multistation conditioning equipment. (Photo courtesy Universal Athletic Sales Co., Fresno, California.)

mum of a hundred square feet is needed per machine. In addition, the popularity of individual exercise machines such as rowers, joggers, vibrators, cycles, and abdominal trimmers mandates that room be provided to house these.

Because of the "heaviness" of the equipment necessary for use in these rooms, reinforced wall mounts and floor installations should be provided. Because physical exertion is implied in activity of this kind, with resulting perspiration of participants, it is essential that adequate ventilation be considered. The room itself should be situated reasonably equidistant to the men's and women's dressing facilities, since on many occasions it will be a shared facility.

The weight training room is one facility that should be permanently installed because it is impractical and in some cases impossible to move the equipment from place to place. Consequently, flooring, ceilings, lighting, acoustics, and ventilation specifications can be developed to deal specifically with the utilization planned for this room. It is generally agreed that a minimum of 2500 square feet is required to accommodate just one class, but this figure depends on the variety and number of machines and equipment contained in the room. A ceiling height of 12 feet is a minimum requirement. Since there is considerable individual endeavor in this room, the installation of a continuous music system is a welcome and gracious appurtenance.

Current educational philosophy regarding handicapped students suggests that they be "mainstreamed," that is, fit into the regular pattern of student life (Fig. 7-7).

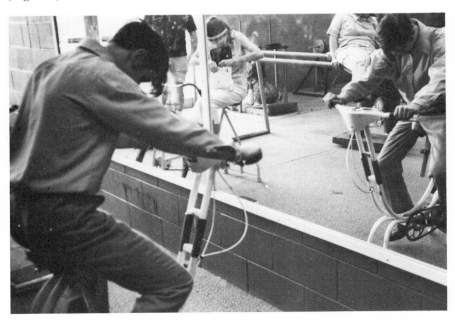

Fig. 7-7. Orange Grove Center for the Trainable Retarded, Chattanooga, Tennessee. (Photo courtesy Educational Facilities Laboratories, Inc.; Larry Molloy, photographer.)

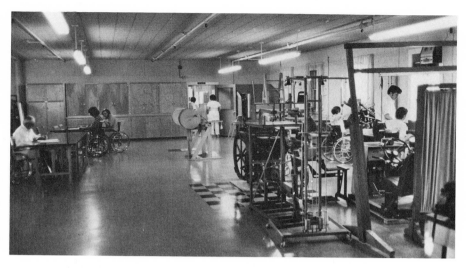

Fig. 7-8. Woodrow Wilson Rehabilitation Center, Fisherville, Virginia. (Photo courtesy Educational Facilities Laboratories, Inc.; Larry Molloy, photographer.)

Equipment for physical therapeutic purposes can easily be installed in the weight training room and used interchangeably and concurrently. For this reason, planners should seriously consider incorporating within the weight training room a therapeutic center where those in need of a therapeutic program can find all they need to pursue such a regimen (Fig. 7-8). Such a room will, of necessity, be bigger and more fully appointed with additional program aids and equipment. Electrical outlets for electrically operated machinery should be carefully and judiciously placed. Implicit in any specifications for a weight training and therapeutic room are adequate facilities for storage and the display of charts and other information necessary for the conduct of the program.

SAUNAS

With the socialization of certain aspects of physical education and particularly with the attention paid to individual programs of physical fitness and figure control for both sexes, saunas have become commonplace. Saunas provide a nice "topping off" to a hard workout, a period of relaxation while experiencing the physiological values purported to accrue to the user. Saunas first became popular in expensive private health clubs, where they were built to accommodate no more than five or six people at a time. In considering saunas for school and community use, however, they should be of sufficient size to accommodate considerably more users at one time. Saunas should be located close to the weight training room and, because of the requirements for water and plumbing, it would be well to consider their location close to the aquatics area or the main shower area. Because of the health club image that saunas create, they should be located where individuals can use them just as easily as a class group.

However, in school situations the medical staff and physical educators should clearly delineate procedures for sauna use, since there are medical conditions for which saunas may present a health hazard.

COMMUNITY ROOM

The community room has commonly and alternately been referred to in the past as the recreational room, game room, or street shoe room. In the terminology of today's education/recreation, this community room now replaces the multipurpose room and acts as a "catchall" for those needs not specifically accommodated in other facilities. (See Fig. 7-9.)

To better understand how to plan, facilitate, and equip this room, it would be best first to have some understanding of what will happen inside it. It will be the place where chairs will be moved in for a fathers' club meeting or for a community "booster club" meeting. The various student committees affiliated with the physical education program will meet here, as will coaching groups and other professional groups. It will serve as a "rap room" for students who spend a lot of time in the gym and also as a reading room or a relaxation lounge between classes. Quiet games such as checkers, cards, and backgammon might be played, and the room might also serve as a place for recreational table tennis. Similarly, it should be able to handle square and folk dancing and can be the site for small musical or dance presentations.

Fig. 7-9. Community Room at LaVerne College, LaVerne, California. (Photo courtesy Educational Facilities Laboratories, Inc.)

Flexibility is the key in planning this special room, which should be easily accessible to the outside; because of its potential around-the-clock utilization, it should be located in such a way as to lock it off from the rest of the building, if necessary. Toilet and light kitchen facilities should be accessible. Storage for chairs, tables, lecterns, and other conference essentials should be provided. The heavy use to which this room is subjected requires a hard floor surfacing that is easily maintained.

The convertible auditorium function that this room serves suggests an adequate size of at least 70 by 100 feet so that a movie screen and projection equipment can be put to maximum use. In consideration of the hard use to which this room will be put, all equipment and furniture should be particularly durable and easily maintained. In addition, because of the reasonably large assemblages expected, ceiling height should be sufficient to avoid a "closed-in" feeling. Proper lighting, acoustics, and ventilation again are of paramount importance in the design of the community room.

FACILITIES FOR SPECIAL POPULATIONS

One of the concomitant effects of the sweeping civil rights legislation enacted in the 1960s and 1970s was the institutionalization of equal rights for all Americans. Every segment of life that in any way comes under federal regulations is now affected. All minority groups—children, women, the poor, racial minorities, the aged, the physically handicapped—have suddenly been covered under an umbrella of new laws governing many everyday activities. A dramatic manifestation of this is the attention that has suddenly been focused on programs of physical education for the handicapped.

Federal and foundation funds have become available for worthwhile programs involving the handicapped. Building codes have been rewritten to accommodate the handicapped, special Olympics have been initiated, and in general attention has been focused on the need to plan for the integration of this special population into the mainstream of American life. Indeed, the term *mainstreaming* has become the catchword of the methodology for education of the handicapped (Fig. 7-10). The accepted policy of most agencies and institutions that serve handicapped populations now is to move firmly in the direction of including the handicapped, wherever possible, in the regular programs and facilities of the rest of the normal population—into the mainstream. No longer do they seek, or does the law tolerate, special rooms or special programs. Instead, provisions have to be made for including the handicapped in all public facilities and programs.

Some basic definitions and explanations are in order. One has to do with terminology. In some programs this population is referred to as *handicapped*, in others, as *disabled*. Some texts speak of *special* children, some of *exceptional* children, and some programs are for *educable* children. In short, although controversy rages among the professionals as to the physical, psychological, emotional, and educational limitations and differences that are distinct and peculiar

95

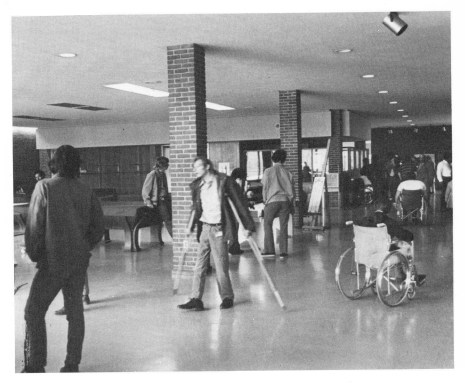

Fig. 7-10. Into the mainstream in school recreation room. (Photo courtesy Educational Facilities Laboratories, Inc.; Larry Molloy, photographer.)

to any group within the handicapped umbrella, there is little doubt that the persons in question are members of a minority group of Americans who might not be able to function within the framework of normal society.

Moreover, prior to the 1970s the term *handicapped student* frequently was used with one frame of reference. It usually meant physically handicapped and frequently was immediately identified with a person in a wheelchair or on crutches. Now it may be clearly understood that the term handicapped (or disabled, or exceptional, or special) refers not only to those who are on crutches or in wheelchairs, but also to those who have impairments in speech, vision, and hearing and those who suffer from heart or mental defects. In some cases persons might be handicapped by advancing age or by other ailments common to the aged population.

Although adequate documentation is not easily available, it is estimated that in the United States alone between 8% and 10% of school-age children are physically handicapped, emotionally disturbed, brain injured, auditorially impaired, or possess chronic health problems. "Seven million school-age children, roughly one out of ten in the United States, are handicapped."[2] It becomes obvious that there are staggering numbers of people whose special needs must be considered and met.

Every physical education or sports facility built in America today should have incorporated into it the essentials that guarantee the handicapped the ease and convenience inherently provided for the nonhandicapped. Most of the appurtenances can be provided without drawing attention to their presence and without inconveniencing the general public. In fact, they generally can be "lost" in good design. The American National Standards Institute has developed clearly stated specifications making buildings accessible to and usable by the handicapped. Their material and the recommendations of other professional associations that serve the handicapped should be considered before embarking on any building program.[1]

To aid the generalist in physical education to be somewhat conversant with the state of the art in planning facilities for the handicapped, some broad considerations follow.

Ramps, doorways, and hallways must be engineered to accommodate wheelchairs. The actual dimensions of wheelchair height, width, and turning space requirements are standard and should be made available to the architect. At least one primary entrance to any sports facility should be a ramp type; more and more, ramps are replacing stairs as attractive and functional ways to enter and exit from any building. In any sports arena, seat areas that are fed by ramps should then have adequate aisle space to accommodate wheelchairs.

The toilet complex of any gymnasium or arena should have facilities clearly delineated for wheelchairs or other physically handicapped people, with toilets, urinals, sinks, and mirrors placed in such a way as to be comfortably used by those in wheelchairs. This implies specific width and height of stalls, outward opening direction of stall doors, and handrails suitably placed to bear the weight of the user. It implies, too, that shelves, soap and towel dispensers, and water fountains be judiciously placed. Telephones should be placed so that they can be easily reached from a wheelchair, and special phones should be provided for those with hearing disabilities and for those who cannot dial manually.

Special provision should be made for food service, vending machines, and locker door openings.

Distinctively shaped doorknobs should be installed on doors leading to areas of potential danger so that the visually handicapped can be aware of such hazards. Raised numerals and signs should be on doors. Electronic devices and bell tones can warn the blind of open doors or other hazards. Large and clearly understandable direction signs should be prominently posted in every sports facility so that those with speech or auditory problems do not have to experience additional difficulty in asking for directions. In fact, audible warning signals should accompany simultaneous visual signals for the benefit of the deaf and the blind.

In gymnasium complexes, and particularly in areas where there is likely to

Fig. 7-11. Specially designed pool at Woodrow Wilson Rehabilitation Center, Fisherville, Virginia. (Photo courtesy Educational Facilities Laboratories, Inc.; Larry Molloy, photographer.)

be water on the floor, floors should have a nonslip surface. Elevator doors should close slowly enough so as not to be a threat to slower-moving handicapped persons, and controls should be placed at a reachable level.

In addition, certain nonessential but gracious accoutrements that show sensitivity to the needs of the handicapped can be built into the facility, such as a bell or musical tone that sounds every hour, hallway indentures where crippled students and those in wheelchairs can stop to rest or talk without encumbering the flow of traffic, or designated phones that can be used if someone is in need of assistance.

These considerations generally apply to spectators, or at least to those not directly involved in participating in programs conducted within the structure. Several accommodations can be made to enable the handicapped student to participate fully in a near normal program, and all special facilities built for special activities should similarly include these adjustments for the handicapped.

Gymnasium floors should be so constructed as to allow the free wheeling of a chair. Wood or durable synthetic surfaces are recommended. Some of the basketball backstops should be adjustable, and specially designed approaches to a bowling alley can permit the blind and those confined to wheelchairs to participate fully. Swimming pools (Fig. 7-11) should have a ramped access area with handrails and guides. Mechanically operated lifts should be available for wheelchair-bound people.

Every activity offered to the general population should be available to the handicapped. The American public is becoming accustomed to seeing more and more "special" groups in the mainstream of society's activities.

REFERENCES

1. American National Standards Institute: Making buildings and facilities accessible to the physically handicapped, publication no. A 117.1, 1430 Broadway, New York, N.Y.
2. Educational Facilities Laboratories: One out of ten, New York, October, 1974.
3. National Association of College Directors of Athletics and American Association of Health, Physical Education and Recreation: Administration of athletics in colleges and universities, Washington, D.C., 1971, The Associations.
4. Planning areas and facilities for HPER-AAHPER and The Athletic Institute, Chicago, 1966, Merchandise Mart.

CHAPTER 8

The service core

The *core area* consists of locker rooms, showers, toilets, laundry rooms, training rooms, equipment rooms, maintenance, storage areas, and space for building mechanicals. These rooms and areas can be placed within the shell of one large space or can be placed in a smaller structure adjacent to the recreation areas. The decision to place the core within one large structure housing all activities or to place it adjacent to a structure or structures housing the sports and activity areas is a local option usually determined by cost. When financial considerations require that a new facility be built in stages, the core is usually an adjacent structure found in the first phase of the building program.

This chapter is divided into nine discussions, each one dealing with a different component of the service core. Because of the many individual and local options available in constructing the service core, several somewhat newer possibilities and innovations have presented themselves. For this reason, after several of the discussions some "Ideas to Kick Around in Class" are given. They are provided to stimulate and promote some class discussion on their feasibility.

LOCKER ROOM

This area in which students change clothes has usually been distinguished by long rows of green, gray, or tan metal lockers. In older facilities an odor associated with the "smells of the gym" is sometimes present as well.

Lockers or small bins can be acquired in sizes ranging from those only small enough to contain shoes, T-shirts, and intimate apparel to those large enough for a person to stand in (Fig. 8-1). The decision on locker style, size, and overall height is a matter of choice based on the number of students using the area at any one time. Rules governing the number of lockers vary from city to city and state to state, with codes specifying numerical formulas. The number and type of lockers is best determined by considering factors such as size of the student body, class size for physical education, number of classes per period, community recreation use, and interscholastic programs. In essence, it is a decision to be arrived at locally and cooperatively. Consideration of traffic flow around the lockers should take into account the number of concurrent users during any given period of the day or night.

The early history of locker rooms and shower facilities may be helpful to present and future administrators. The earliest facilities were built many years ago when indoor plumbing was not common in homes; thus the public facilities in the school were planned and installed for reasons of health. The times dictated bathtubs, which were later replaced by showers. Women were afforded private dressing cubicles. From this very simple, logical arrangement the ulti-

Fig. 8-1. A, Locker room, PER Center, SUNY, Cortland, New York. **B,** William Woods College locker room, Fulton, Missouri.

mate locker room has developed into an expensive clubhouse with locker stalls large enough to sit in, carpeted floors, clubhouse attendants, and lush lounge areas. Institutional locker rooms run the gamut between these two extremes of simplicity and luxurious sophistication (Fig. 8-2).

An analysis of functions of the early locker room related to today's society and projected patterns of future student use should be made. As stated previously, the locker room, by definition, is a place to change from daily attire to

Fig. 8-2. Locker room of the St. Louis Cardinals Baseball Club, Busch Stadium. (Photo by Dave Spilver.)

recreational clothing. In the institutional setting the room is usually an expedient to get a person to the recreational or activity area and back to class. It is a minimum-time facility. Consequently, before spending monies on any facilities, time-usage studies should be made. If students spend fifty minutes in a gymnasium and ten minutes in a locker room, the cost-time factor of these two areas should be reflected in the amount of money spent for each.

In a large area set aside for a locker room the lockers may be any color. There is usually no added expense for bright colors. Color coding can then become a factor in the administration of the area. There is no law stating that lockers must be lined up in long military rows. In some cases they have been effectively arranged into rectangular geometric shapes to accommodate visiting teams or varsity teams. In other institutions they have been placed into swastika-like patterns to control traffic and vandalism. Cage doors may be placed between areas to afford greater security. Liberalizing forces in today's society question the necessity of dressing cubicles for women. Dressing stalls have become obsolete.

Carpeting can be an asset or a detriment, depending on the maintenance staff and funds available. If projections for the future indicate a lack of staff and inability to repair mechanical equipment, carpeting then becomes a health hazard, and replacement funds for new carpeting become questionable. It does offer an acoustical advantage. An easily cleaned nonslick surface is preferable.

Mirrors should be placed on posts and at the end of locker rows. Hair dryers should be placed in all locker rooms. Once again a careful count study is in order.

The use of graffiti-type wall markings to direct people with large colorful signs and arrows has proved successful. In addition to graffiti, colored lockers, bright floor patterns, and alert personnel are assets. Use the basic mechanicals (ducts, pipes, beams) to further enliven the locker room area and reduce construction costs. False walls and ceiling add to the cost. They do not enhance the basic function of the area and on many occasions offer opportunities for vandalism. Many commercial complexes and institutions have used these approaches in a positive manner for educational purposes. Visit institutions that have done this successfully.

Ideas to kick around in class. Are mobile locker rooms feasible? . . . Locker cells in a lounge setting? . . . Prefabricated locker rooms? . . . Cabana concept for both sexes? . . . Coed locker room (coed dormitories exist)? . . . Locker room lounge? . . . Food in the locker room? . . . Locker room traffic patterns? . . . Advantages and disadvantages of private locker rooms for varsity teams . . . Using existing locker space for visiting teams . . . Accessibility of equipment to locker room . . . Team trunks . . . Training tables . . . Chalkboards . . . Handicapped traffic . . . Locker room and shower modules.

SHOWER ROOM

The number of shower heads relates directly to the number of lockers, the maximum number of students who are expected to shower within a given time, and the number who actually do shower. A rule of thumb is a six student-to-one shower ratio.

It must be remembered that in the early 1970s the high costs of plumbing installations and the "rule of thumb formulas" resulted in showers being built that were rarely if ever used. Shower rooms were built according to codes of the early 1930s for people in the 1980s. With the plumbing technology available today, sound planning should go into the number and type of showers to be built. A deck shower should be specified at all indoor and outdoor swimming areas. Shower heads should be wall- or post-mounted on the deck of the pool. When a less expensive shower solution is specified, more funds are available for the activity areas.

Shower heads placed on the wall of the shower room offer full use of four walls. Plumbing problems, however, often necessitate removing a part of the wall to make repairs as problems of age set in. This type of installation also presents problems of maintenance in relationship to renovation and difficulty in cleaning the walls because of the presence of pipes and wall openings. Obviously a plain wall is preferable. A wall and floor surface that does not require painting or plaster repair is ideal.

The post shower with multiple heads placed in the center of the room offers several options (Fig. 8-3). In the event of a plumbing malfunction the sleeve on the post can be removed and the repairs made. All walls remain clear of any obstacles, which facilitates cleaning. Fins and shower curtains may be attached to a post shower in the event this is deemed necessary. Current trends indicate gang showers in all shower rooms. Those who seek the privacy of personal stalls use their own living accommodations or those of friends.

103

Fig. 8-3. Men's shower room in Richards Building, Brigham Young University, Provo, Utah.

Individual shower handles that may also be reached by the handicapped are preferable. Two handles, one for hot and one for cold, serve to complicate plumbing, increase costs, and increase the odds on needed repairs. The single-handle shower is preferable but must be clearly marked and color coded for water temperature selection.

Soap is a matter of individual preference. Containers fastened to the wall become objects for play and vandalism. Bar soap remains the simplest solution causing the fewest problems.

The total enclosure of the "shower room" is the basis of many locker room and shower room problems. The wall adjacent to the locker room or drying room area can at times be eliminated or terminated at a height of approximately 4 feet, affording greater openness and administrative control of an area.

Ideas to kick around in class. Shower posts placed throughout the locker room . . . Individual locker rooms each with a centered post shower . . . Roman baths versus gang showers . . . Which activities dictate a need for showers? . . . Central shower house.

EQUIPMENT ROOM

Equipment storage space for personal and "in season" sports equipment can be a separate room or several rooms. Dead storage for out-of-season gear is preferred in separate areas, or the two can be combined. Wall space should be shelved with bins and cabinets to contain what is referred to as the "whites," towels and personal gear. Sports equipment for classes and games must be within easy reach. A determination of the amount of space needed can be calculated exactly by using the checklist for space and equipment in Appendixes A and B. A volume and square foot area determined for all occupants in the structure can then help determine whether it is advisable to have additional storage rooms for out-of-season gear.

The program determines the size and proximity of the equipment area. The exact geographical location within the structure is further determined by traffic patterns as they relate to indoor sports, outdoor sports, the laundry, availability to delivery, and both sexes. It should be a closed room with double-door access because screen walls are easily cut, and soft materials become accessible by fishing through the mesh.

Storage room security is an unpleasant reality that must be faced. All walls must rise to structural materials above, either roof or upper floors. Artificial ceilings are easily removed, providing for entrance into the equipment area and encouraging theft. The equipment room is a desirable target for many because it contains materials that students prize; therefore security is a serious consideration.

A counter area for repair and maintenance of equipment should be placed in the room. Renovation cost should be figured early in the planning process.

LAUNDRY ROOM

A laundry room is not essential in all schools but must be considered at the secondary and higher education levels. Towels, socks, T-shirts, shorts, swimming suits, and many other items should be laundered daily if satisfactory health standards are to be maintained. The latest commercial equipment makes it feasible for institutional personnel to operate all equipment.

The clean equipment must be accessible to the area where it is to be dispensed to the students, usually the equipment room. At the same time the equipment room must be accessible so that collection of dirty equipment does not become an impossible problem. If dressing areas are on several floors, gathering of dirty equipment can be accommodated by chutes, collection centers, or cleverly planned student traffic patterns. However, moving clean laundry from one level to another becomes more complicated. First choice dictates an elevator accessible to both the laundry room and the equipment room. Second choice is a ramping system, which may also be used by handicapped students.

The room itself should be a plain structure, made of concrete or some similar basic material, attended by the necessary gas and electrical lines. Water lines and drains must be available. In an effort to reduce costs the core areas requiring plumbing facilities can be located in adjacent areas. Counter tops and tables for sorting equipment are desirable, but it may be a duplication of space and equipment if there is counter space in the equipment room.

Ideas to kick around in class. Have paper goods been perfected to a point rendering a laundry obsolete? . . . Is it cheaper to contract laundering of heavy practice and game equipment to an outside firm? . . . Should there be a degree program that trains specialists in equipment purchase, maintenance, and repair?

MAINTENANCE AREAS (CUSTODIAL)

A central maintenance area containing an office and communications system for maintenance personnel should be provided in the core area. This does not minimize the fact that there must be rooms and large vented closets in each sector of the building. The personnel responsible for maintaining the building cannot be expected to spend a large part of their time toting heavy equipment up and down stairs or over great distances. Each area must have water and sinks available, electrical outlets, and storage cupboards for paper supplies and cleaning supplies. Built-in racks should be provided for brushes and mops. In a multifloor building without an elevator, heavy equipment and space for storage should be provided on each floor.

VARSITY TEAM ROOMS

The varsity team room is a dressing area used exclusively for a particular group of athletes involved in a particular sport, usually the "varsity" team. Rooms vary from simple geometric shapes with clothing hooks on the wall and benches around the perimeter of the area to lavishly furnished rooms with sit-in lockers, carpeting, complete plumbing facilities, stereo and audiovisual components, food facilities, and private offices. The extent of the furnishings are determined by the philosophy and the program of the institution. The room for varsity sports should be easily accessible to training, laundry, and equipment rooms.

The design should afford protection of an individual's possessions and team equipment. Special keys attached to large objects should be mandatory.

Ideas to kick around in class. Space allotted to a varsity team should be so designed that it may be used by others when not being used by the assigned team.

TRAINING ROOM

The training and first aid room is an area where the trainer and school physician can provide medical services, preventive and corrective, to all students. It must be able to accommodate laboratory sections of first aid classes and service community groups. In reality, it has to be a series of rooms if it is intended to accommodate both sexes simultaneously. The head trainer's office must be equipped with files to carefully record all treatment. The team physician's office must be large enough for consultation services. Both offices and the room for all therapeutic machines must be coordinated with the school health program. A duplication of equipment for ambulatory athletes is an unnecessary expense.

Fig. 8-4. Training room for men's and women's intercollegiate athletics, SUNY, Cortland, New York.

The basic area contains plinths (a type of medical table for examinations and therapeutic exercises), whose number will vary according to the size of the student body (Fig. 8-4). All cabinets for supplies and taping tables may be in this area or in an adjacent area, depending on peak load traffic. Electrical outlets should be available to each unit in the area. Complete plumbing facilities and floor drains must be accessible in each area.

Hydrotherapy units placed in a separate room afford privacy for individuals undergoing treatment. Individual whirlpool units are desirable, and curtains can provide privacy if desired.

The entire area should be accessible to all students without being in the main traffic flow. In locating the training area, varsity team locations must be considered because of the excessive amount of preventive taping required for varsity athletes. Access to ambulance service must be considered when egress is considered.

Six basic areas must be planned for general first aid and taping, electrotherapy, hydrotherapy, offices, storage, and exercise areas. A conference room can be built into the core medical area or placed adjacent to it. The steam room and sauna bath need not be built into the area, since these generally will be used for recreation purposes. Administratively, however, they should fall into the first aid area.

An additional room, the visiting team training room, should be considered if visiting team rooms are so designed that plinths and taping tables cannot be placed there. It must serve additional functions during the times when there are no contests scheduled.

Ideas to kick around in class. One major area versus several small areas . . . Men and women trainers working together . . . Visiting teams using the home institution's trainers . . . Upgrading the training profession to the ethical codes of the medical profession . . . Encouraging coaches of opposing teams to share home team trainers . . . Assignment of a home trainer to the opposing team . . . Problems involved when the coach is also the trainer . . . Liability and legal responsibilities of any person giving medical assistance to a student . . . Professional training program for student aides.

TOWELING OR DRYING AREA

The toweling area is the space allotted for hanging a towel prior to entering a shower room and the area in which a person dries on leaving the shower room. A rule of thumb for a utopian facility states that the area should be the same size as the shower room to prevent water from being tracked throughout the facility. Unless a security person is present to prevent it, the space allotted for drying is in effect a hallway through which one proceeds to the dressing area. Given class schedules and the fast tempo of educational life, the toweling area does not serve the intended purpose and constitutes a valuable loss of space and dollars. Towel hooks and racks can be effectively placed inside the shower room and on the exterior walls of the room. A drain should be placed at each entrance to the shower room and a nonskid floor material provided.

REST ROOMS

Toilet facilities must be conveniently placed adjacent to all areas—locker rooms, shower rooms, training rooms, spectator facilities, and main traffic arteries. Extensive plumbing facilities account for the single most expensive item in a facility, so a careful study of the projected use of the area should be concluded before decisions are made as to the number and placement of toilet facilities. At one famous institution there were two and a half toilets for each student. By this formula, a family of four would require ten bathrooms.

If large banks of rest room facilities can be placed adjacent to the main locker room areas and also adjacent to the traffic areas for spectator events, a steel dividing door can be used, affording the dressing facilities a limited number of units and allowing the others for the public. During spectator events dressing areas are at a low peak period. In this manner the units are able to do double duty. If a usable arrangement can be devised, there should be two water closets, two hand lavatories, and two urinals for the first twenty-five people. For each additional twenty students one urinal and one lavatory should be added. For each additional twenty-five people one water closet should be added.

Ideas to kick around in class. Are urinals necessary? . . . Can a unit be designed to accommodate both sexes and eliminate the urinal? . . . Where does the air dryer belong? . . . If roll paper towels are adequate in the toilet area, can similar items be introduced in the shower area?

CHAPTER 9

The academic core

OFFICE AND ADMINISTRATIVE UNITS

Administrative areas must be designed in harmony with the basic program as outlined by the institution. Offices and support areas reflect the philosophy of the institution, regardless of academic level. All recommendations relayed to the architects will vary according to age level and intensity of proposed usage by the clientele. The functions of professional staff must be clearly delineated, so that the facilities to accommodate them and their roles can be tailored accordingly. For example, the role of athletic director of a major university is exclusively that of an executive administrator, which requires a corporate style office facility. On the other hand, the athletic director in a typical junior high school is an all-in-one staff of teacher, coach, counselor, and administrator, which requires an office combination to accommodate these functions.

Therefore a series of vague "rule of thumb" formulas and checklists should be reviewed as the plans for administrative space progress from the institutional philosophy through specifications, schematic drawings, preliminary drawings, and into working drawings. Each step requires an administrative checkback into the original goals to be sure that they are being met.

As a starting point in planning for adequate administrative units, a "rule of thumb" formula suggests that the total number of users be divided by 275. For example, this formula would require a minimum of ten administrative units for a student enrollment of 2750. As physical education requirements have declined in higher education, recreation–leisure time programs have increased. Each has offset the other, but facility utilization figures remain the same. In academic credit–oriented programs one secretary for three full-time staff members is deemed desirable. Each full-time staff member should have an individual working space. Although recommended, the formula just given is rarely adhered to by private educational institutions at any level. Unfortunately, public education is beginning to emulate private education in this respect. No office should be less than a hundred square feet in size, and each should be appointed in a manner that provides an inviting work area in which to grade papers, prepare lecture and research materials, and most important, to counsel students. Customary equipment consists of a desk with a lock, a chair, shelves to accommodate several hundred books, an additional chair, and a four-drawer file cabinet with a lock. The physical aspects of the area should encourage the staff member and students to decorate the area as pleasantly as possible. More staff and student hours will be spent in the office units than in the activity areas. Avoid unattractive colors that have an institutional look. An uninviting office area discourages use by faculty and students alike.

ADMINISTRATIVE SUPPORT AREAS

Duplicating and stenographic space with the attendant supplies should be convenient to all secretaries and accessible to the professional staff. This room should be supervised by the office manager or a designee so that it is not misused by unauthorized personnel. At institutions where the staff is small all staff members should be trained in the operation of the duplicating equipment so that valuable administrative and secretarial time is not lost in locating a trained operator.

THE LOUNGE

The lounge, mail room, and general staff area serve several useful functions in terms of generating dialogue among faculty members, faculty and staff, and administration. The formal seminar or conference room by design imposes a severity that eliminates informal talk and the easy give-and-take essential to a healthy working atmosphere.

THE LIBRARY

Controversy rages over the wisdom of developing separate professional libraries for specific subject areas in undergraduate institutions. At the graduate level a highly professional subject area library is a necessity. An unnecessary expenditure occurs when the main campus library duplicates volumes found in the physical education department library. Campus libraries should be designed to accommodate all the students in an institution, and study carrels should be provided with all multimedia materials available. The physical education and recreation department has the obligation to see that the main campus library contains all relevant volumes and materials for its students. Every student should be encouraged to make use of the latest materials in the visual media field and should learn to operate all the equipment. Library and multimedia equipment usage is clearly a function of the professional in the ranks of physical education and recreation. Physical education has been the vestibule through which much educational hardware has been introduced into the mainstream of academic use. Instant videotape replay machines, overhead projectors, and instructional films were first used by coaches to improve their teaching techniques and were then absorbed into the mainstream of academic life.

CLASSROOMS

Any institution with a major sports program, a major recreational/physical education program, or a combination of both plus related areas should have a minimum of three well-equipped classrooms. Each classroom should be equipped with 220 and 110 voltage outlets in the floor, chalkboards, movie screens, and television monitors. The largest room should contain enough seats to accommodate the single largest unit of students. It also should be divisible into smaller units as desired. Classrooms are much more suitable for meetings

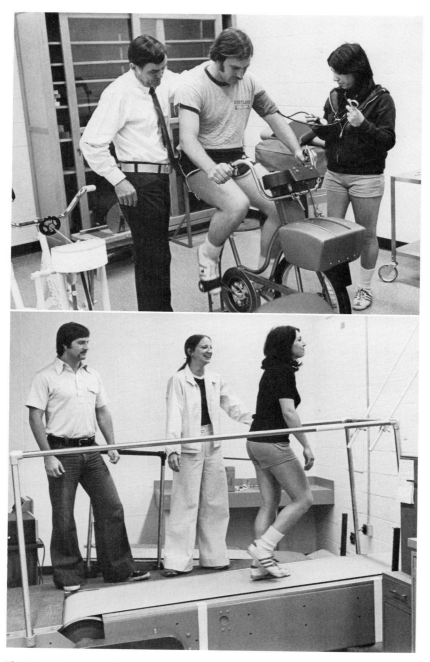

Fig. 9-1. Human Performance Laboratory, PER Center, SUNY, Cortland, New York.

than are laboratories, where expensive and usually movable equipment becomes a problem.

THE LABORATORY

The need for a physical education laboratory or laboratories plus the additional interest generated in the research areas of biomechanics has created serious budgetary problems for those institutions involved in serious graduate study and research. Effective research tends to be diluted as class sizes are increased and existing facilities overtaxed; thus careful planning for laboratory space is mandated. (See Fig. 9-1.)

Following are some questions that must be faced by institutions contemplating the construction of laboratories in the face of a decline in potential students:

Can universities afford to pay faculty members for research-related time?

Are unintentional intracampus departmental conflicts creating duplication of expensive laboratory facilities and equipment on the same campus?

Are basic knowledge areas duplicated so that major concepts may be contained in one lecture section and specialized interests effectively dealt with in laboratory sessions?

Are there existing laboratories on campus in which physical therapy, biomechanics, and other sciences could be taught if more effective administrative scheduling were practiced?

Before constructing a facility that could easily become a monument to one research-oriented individual, it is essential to review the curriculum, projected departmental goals, and university growth patterns and master plans. Review the types of laboratories involved in physical education and determine those which would be an asset in the physical education/recreation facility. Basic equipment lists in the laboratories must be checked against an inventory of equipment in existing campus laboratories. Research methods and equipment change rapidly, thereby creating the necessity for a continuous dialogue among those on the campus engaged in research. One laboratory correctly equipped may well serve several different courses.

CHAPTER 10

Swimming pools

Milton A. Gabrielsen, Ph.D.*

The rate of construction of swimming pools in the United States in the twenty-year period between 1954 and 1974 was nothing short of phenomenal. From an estimated 28,000 pools in 1954, the figure reached the staggering total of over 5 million by the end of 1974.[6] Of equal interest is the fact that 85% of this total represents residential-type pools and of that number, a majority are above-ground pools (sometimes referred to as portable pools). It has been estimated that as many as 50 million Americans swim in some type of pool facility on a hot Saturday or Sunday in the summer. The phenomenal growth in interest in swimming was similarly spurred by the incredible growth of other water-related sports such as boating, water skiing, scuba diving, fishing, and sailing, which all require the safety component that swimming provides.

Two factors have contributed most to the growth in pool construction: first, the tremendous technological improvements in all aspects of swimming pool construction, including equipment, filtration methods, chemical water treatment, and enclosures for pools, and second, the increase in discretionary income of Americans, which, coupled with the recreation and population explosion after World War II, created a climate most favorable to recreational pursuits.

Today there is scarcely a community of 10,000 population that does not have a pool. Some of these are highly sophisticated facilities, which have gone beyond the single all-purpose pool so common in the past to aquatic complexes numbering as many as five pools, each serving a particular function (Fig. 10-1). Schools—elementary, high school, and college—have also experienced a boom in development of pools as a part of their physical education and school recreation programs (Fig. 10-2).

The recognition by school and community officials that swimming is probably the most popular form of recreation with all age groups and yields tremendous value in relationship to capital expenditure has undoubtedly spurred the development of pools in this country. Most community pools constructed in the past twenty years have been outdoor pools, whereas most school and college pools have been built as part of the indoor physical education plant. Recent trends indicate that more and more communities are beginning to construct indoor pools to meet the demand of people for year-round swimming programs (Fig. 10-3). For years it was assumed that people were not as interested in

*Dr. Milton A. Gabrielsen, Professor Emeritus, New York University, is currently Director of Studies in Human Habitability at Nova University in Florida. Dr. Gabrielsen is a long-time member of the Board of Directors and consultant to the Council for National Cooperation in Aquatics.

113

Fig. 10-1. Three–swimming pool complex in the Village of Scarsdale, New York.

Fig. 10-2. William Woods College Pool, Fulton, Missouri.

swimming in the winter months as during the hot summer season. It was probably true in the past; however, with the construction of attractive indoor pools housed in buildings that provide a multiplicity of recreation activities, swimming has emerged as a year-round sport. And yet in 1974 only an estimated 3% of public schools in this country had pools. Gymnasiums still remain the first physical education facility built, in spite of mounting evidence that if the decision were left up to the students, the majority would vote that the pool should

Fig. 10-3. Community pool at Columbia, Maryland, showing vinyl removable roof covering.

be built before the gym. The influence of basketball on physical education programs is still the dominant factor in planning school physical education and recreation facilities.

This chapter cannot deal in any depth with all the aspects involved in planning and designing a pool. Thus the purpose of this chapter is to outline the basic elements related to planning, design, and operation of pools and suggest sources for additional guidance and information. It is hoped that the "current status of the art" will be provided the reader. The most comprehensive source of information on swimming pools currently available is a book sponsored by the Council for National Cooperation in Aquatics (CNCA), *Swimming Pools— A Guide to their Planning, Design, and Operation.*[2]

PLANNING FOR A POOL

For every community pool project planned by a citizen's group, a recreation department, or a board of education, only one out of four is successfully completed. This is not a good batting average. Why do so many of these projects fail to become a reality? Inadequate planning, poor timing, and poor promotion appear to be the main causes. It is true, however, that subsequently many of these defeated projects eventually succeed, usually on the second or third attempt.

The specific procedures employed in planning a pool will inevitably vary among agencies (schools and colleges) and municipalities. Nevertheless, many common elements in the planning process apply to any agency, regardless of sponsorship. Agencies would do well to use the steps outlined here as a guide in their planning.

Establishing the need. Unless there is a demonstrated need for a swimming pool, as revealed by such evidence as a strong mandate from the people or the result of a study of the number of available pools in the community or both, the likelihood of getting approval from a board of education, college board of trustees, or a city council is rather slim. The matter of determining the availability of support for the operation of the pool once it has been built must also be established. One person or a small committee should be given the responsibility for coordinating the pool project, which initially includes not only the matter of determining need but also preparing the "program design." This represents a statement of the program requirements and specifications for the pool. The statement should include the following:

- A list of activities to be conducted in the pool, that is, instruction of beginners (give age), recreation swimming, lifesaving, competition swimming, scuba diving instruction, water polo, swimming for the handicapped, diving, water shows, etc.
- A general description of the pool, locating it in relationship to other facilities; also, the number of users
- Type and size of administrative facilities-offices and storage rooms
- Equipment, both instructional and fixed
- Specific requirements and specifications for each activity to be conducted, including anticipated pool use, age of users, size of water oar needed, rules governing activity, water depth needed, length and width of pool, height of ceiling, and identification of any special equipment and facilities needed

Study other pools. By visiting pools recently constructed, particularly those of outstanding quality, much can be learned about the latest pool tech-

Fig. 10-4. University of Tennessee's outdoor 50-meter pool with indoor 50-meter pool in background.

nology and operating practices, including the annual cost of operating a pool. This should be a function of the planning committee or the individual assigned to the project. They might also study carefully all applicable state and local laws pertaining to swimming pools, as well as published professional standards. The specific requirements for conducting competitive swimming and diving meets as well as other aquatic activities are best determined by reference to rule books published by the various governing authorities such as the National Collegiate Athletic Association (NCAA), Amateur Athletic Union (AAU), and Federation of State High School Associations. (See Fig. 10-4.)

Use of pool consultant. A qualified pool consultant often may save an agency considerable time and money. Such a consultant can be extremely helpful in the first two steps just outlined if engaged at the beginning of the project. A consultant may be hired by the contracting agency or the architectural or engineering firm engaged to plan the pool and eventually should be responsible for preparing the "program design" for the pool. This professional brings an expertise to the project that assures that the latest trends in pool technology are applied.

Engagement of architect or pool engineer. Some public agencies are required by law to engage an architectural firm for preparation of construction plans. In many states engineering firms are also approved as authorized pool designers. In a few instances in which the law does not require the employment of an architect, agencies have prepared several plans and "performance specifications" and requested bids from firms that specialize in pool construction. This approach can save money, provided the person preparing the "performance specification" is highly qualified. The pool company has the engineering service necessary to obtain board of health approval.

Fig. 10-5. Pool at Kibbutz Gvat, Haifa, Israel. (Photo courtesy Max Galpaz, architect.)

There is little doubt that the best pool results when the combination of a pool consultant, an architect experienced in pool planning, and a pool engineer are employed. When an architect is used, several firms should be interviewed, at which time evidence of their competency in the area of pool building can be established. The functions of the architect include site analysis, preparation of preliminary plans and cost estimates, development of construction plans, submission of plans to bid, and supervision of construction. The architect also assures the owner that the pool meets all safety standards and local health and building code regulations governing pools. (See Fig. 10-5.)

DESIGN AND CONSTRUCTION CRITERIA

Following are some principles or criteria based on years of experience and research that will assure construction of a modern swimming pool when applied in the planning of any new pool.

Planning

- The specific requirements dictated by the activities to be conducted should serve as criteria for establishing the dimensions and overall design of the pool.
- Whenever possible, people should enter pools from the locker room at the shallow end of the pool. As a safety measure, the water depth should be inscribed in tile or painted on the deck or coping of the pool, where it may readily be seen by those entering the pool.
- The instructor's or director's office should have a direct view of the entire pool area. The office window should be large and made of shatter-proof glass or clear plastic with an opaque blind or curtain to give privacy when desired.
- The filter room should be so located and equipped with locking devices that swimmers do not have access to it. The room should not be used for any other purpose such as storage of cleaning gear, suits, or starting blocks.
- Reflection of outside light on the water in indoor pools is a condition that must be guarded against. Clear glass windows should not be installed on the south or west sides of the pool room. Tinted glass helps reduce the sun's glare and reflection, but in most situations sliding opaque drapes of plastic or fiberglass material should be installed to cover windows.
- A serious problem that must be overcome in indoor pools is condensation. Good ventilation and proper insulation of walls, ceilings, and windows offer the best control of condensation.
- Proper orientation of the pool and bathhouse in outdoor pool complexes is important. Experience has shown that the bathhouse should always be located on the side, where it may help block prevailing winds. Canvas hung on a fence, glass or masonry walls, and plantings may also serve as windbreaks.
- When diving boards are included, the dimensional standards adapted by competitive swimming bodies should be strictly adhered to (Fig. 10-6). The spoon-shaped "diving hopper" can be dangerous, particularly to the inexperienced diver, because it does not provide sufficient depth of water forward from the springboard.

Design

- Providing the proper depth of water and adequate depth markings is one of the most important design factors.
- The amount of deck space in indoor pools should equal the water surface area. Thus a 75- by 35-foot pool should have a deck area of between 2500 and 3000

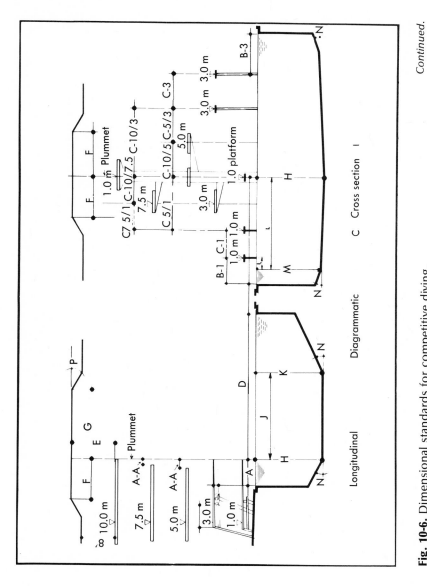

Fig. 10-6. Dimensional standards for competitive diving. (Courtesy R. Jackson Smith.)

Continued.

FINA International Amateur Swimming and Diving Federation

Dimensions for diving facilities

Jan. 1, 1969

		1-meter springboard	3-meter springboard	1-meter platform	3-meter platform	5-meter platform	7.5-meter platform	10-meter platform
Length		16'	16'	15'	16'	20'	20'	20'
Width		1'-8"	1'-8"	1'-8"	2'-6"	5'	5'	6'-6"
Height		3'-3"	9'-10"	3'-3"	9'-10"	16'-4"	24'-7"	32'-10"
A From plummet back to pool wall	Des	A-1	A-3	A-1 (pl)	A-3 (pl)	A-5	A-7.5	A-10
	Min	5'	5'	4'	4'	4'	5'	5'
	(Pref)	(6')	(6')			5'		
A-A From plummet back to platform directly below	Des					AA 5/1	AA-7.5/3 AA-	AA-10/5
	Min					2'-6"	2'-6"	2'-6"
	(Pref)					5'	5'	5'
B From plummet to pool wall at side	Des	B-1	B-3	B-1 (pl)	B-3 (pl)	B-5	B-7.5	B-10
	Min	8'	12'	7'-6"	9'-6"	14'	15'	17'
	(Pref)							
C From plummet to adjacent plummet	Des	C-1	C-3 / C-3/1			C-5/3 / C-5/1	C-7.5/3 / C-7.5/1	C-10/3 / C-10/5
	Min	6'	6'			7'	7'	9'
	(Pref)	(8')	(8')			7'	9'	9'
D From plummet to pool wall ahead	Des	D-1	D-3	D-1 (pl)	D-3 (pl)	D-5	D-7.5	D-10
	Min	29'	34'	26'	31'	34'	36'	45'
	(Pref)							
E Plummet, from board to ceiling overhead	Des	E-1	E-3	E-1 (pl)	E-3 (pl)	E-5	E-7.5	E-10
	Min	16'	16'	10'	10'	10'	10'-6"	
	(Pref)							
F Clear overhead, behind and each side plummet	Des	F-1	F-3	F-1 (pl)	F-3 (pl)	F-5	F-7.5	F-10
	Min	8'	8'	9'	9'	9'	9'	9'
	(Pref)	16'	16'			10'	10'-6"	
G Clear overhead, ahead of plummet	Des	G-1	G-3	G-1 (pl)	G-3 (pl)	G-5	G-7.5	G-10
	Min	16'	16'	16'	16'	16'	16'	20'
	(Pref)	16'	16'			10'	10'-6"	
H Depth of water at plummet	Des	H-1	H-3	H-1 (pl)	H-3 (pl)	H-5	H-7.5	H-10
	Min		12'			12'	13'-6"	15'
	(Pref)	(12')	(13')			13'	15'	16'
J-K Distance, depth of water, ahead of plummet	Des	J-1 K-1	J-3 K-3	J/K-1(pl)	J/K-3(pl)	J-5 K-5	J-7.5 K-7.5	J-10 K-10
	Min	20' 10'-9"	20' 11'-9"	16'/10'-9" 20'/10'-9"	20'/10'-9"	20' 11'-9"	26' 13'	40' 14'
	(Pref)	11'-9"	12'-9"			12'-9"		15'
L-M Distance and depth of water, each side of plummet	Des	L-1 M-1	L-3 M-3	L/M-1(pl)	L/M-3(pl)	L-5 M-5	L-7.5 M-7.5	L-10 M-10
	Min	8' 10'-9"	10'-6" 11'-9"	7'/10'-9" 9'/10'-9"	9'/10'-9"	14' 11'-9"	15' 13'	17' 14'
	(Pref)	11'-9"	12'-9"			12'-9"		15'

N Maximum angle of slope to reduce dimension:	Pool bottom	30 degrees (approximately 1 foot vertical to 2 feet horizontal)
P beyond full requirements:	Ceiling height	30 degrees

Fig. 10-6, cont'd. For legend see p. 119.

square feet. In outdoor pools the deck area plus any lounging areas should be equal to a minimum of four times the water surface area.

- Spectator areas should be separated from the pool by a wall or glass partition. This prevents spectators from getting wet and keeps dirt and debris from the pool deck (Fig. 10-7). In outdoor pools bleachers should be located so that the sun will be on the back of the spectators in the afternoon.

- The distance separating diving boards, when more than one board is installed, is an important safety feature.

- Where a recessed type of gutter is used (not the roll-out or deck level), a *coping* should be provided to prevent debris from washing into the pool.

- Proper lighting of indoor pools is important. At eye level a minimum of 100 footcandles of illumination should be provided. Underwater lights are more for aesthetic effect than safety except in deep-water pools, where they help illuminate the bottom.

- For most effective circulation of water the pump should be placed below the level of the pool. This avoids the need to prime the pump.

- Noise in indoor pools can be minimized by the use of moisture-resistant acoustical material on the ceiling and on at least one wall (Fig. 10-8). Two would be better.

- It is desirable to have the base of the wall of indoor pools coved to facilitate cleaning. Coved ceramic tile and glazed brick are available on the market.

- Gutters, or what is now referred to as the *rimflow system*, should not be thought of only as devices of water circulation. There are many types and shapes of gutters; hence utility should be combined with such factors as appearance, cost, ease of getting in and out of the pool, program requirements, and pool maintenance. The "roll-out" and "level-deck" types of rimflow systems seem to meet most of these criteria.

- The height of the ceiling immediately above diving boards is an important safety factor. A minimum of 15 feet of overhead clearance (from the surface of the

Fig. 10-7. Spectator area is well-defined and controlled at the George Williams College pool.

Fig. 10-8. Attractive soundproofing treatment on upper walls and ceiling at the pool at Mercersburg Academy in Pennsylvania. (Photo courtesy The Eggers Partnership.)

board) is recommended. Thus a pool with a 1-meter board would have a ceiling 18 feet high, and a pool with a 3-meter board would have a ceiling height of 25 feet.

- The pool's outlet should be of sufficient size to enable the pool to be drained in four hours or less.
- Chlorine gas is dangerous; therefore the chlorinator must be located in a room separated from the filter room that contains an exhaust fan located near the floor to clear the room of escaping chlorine gas in the event a leak should occur.
- The depth of the water at various parts of the pool must be properly displayed to prevent accidents that might occur because of a person diving into too shallow water. The best location for depth markings is on the deck or coping of the pool. The markings should be 6 inches high in black or red.
- The deck of an outdoor pool should entirely surround the pool and should be 10 to 20 feet wide, depending on the size of the pool. The larger the pool, the wider the decks.
- The bathhouse or locker room must be properly ventilated to avoid mildew, fungus, and odors collecting in the room.

Construction

- Construction material for decks and pool basin should be evaluated in terms of serviceability, durability, cost, and safety.
- Pipes leading to and from the pool should be located so that they are readily accessible in the event of needed repairs. The use of trenches and integral gutter systems are methods that eliminate the problem of buried pipes.

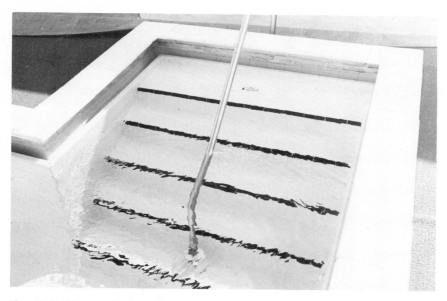

Fig. 10-9. Well-marked steps still offer the best method of exit from a pool.

Fig. 10-10. Swimming pool at U.S. Military Academy, West Point, New York. (Photo courtesy American Olean Tile Co., Lansdale, Pennsylvania.)

- Eyebolts for installation of surface swimming lanes or life lines should be recessed so that they do not protrude from the pool wall or gutter.
- It is best to include a conduit for wiring a public address system during the initial electrical installation to eliminate tearing into walls later.
- Corrosion of pipes and metal fittings can be a problem, particularly in indoor pools. Both humidity and chlorine vapor adversely affect metal; therefore doors, lockers, pipes, grills, diving standards, and other metal fittings should be made of nonferrous metals.
- It is essential from the standpoint of safety that the *deck* around the pool and the floor in the shower room be finished with nonslip material. Slippery decks constitute one of the major sources of accidents.
- The interior of the pool room should be finished in a light color to provide a cheerful, pleasant atmosphere.

Equipment

- Exit from the pool is best accomplished by steps that are set back in the wall or recessed (Fig. 10-9). Steps or ladders should never be placed on the walls in a competitive swimming lane.
- At least one drinking fountain should be located in the pool area. It, too, should be recessed into the wall.
- Bottom lane markers for competitive swimming should be permanently installed, not painted. Ceramic nonslip tile embedded flush in the concrete surface provides the best solution, as it does for turning boards (Fig. 10-10).
- Water slides should not be installed in any public pool, unless they are placed in deep water and strictly supervised.

Operation and administration

- Filters and pumps must be of proper size to produce the desired rate of flow of the pool's water. Most state boards of health require a water turnover rate of eight hours. A more desirable rate of turnover is six hours, and some heavily used pools are geared to a four-hour turnover.
- A safelight should be installed at the entrance of the pool from the locker or shower room. This light should be on whenever the pool is not in use.
- All radiators or heating units used in indoor pools that are within reach of swimmers should be covered and recessed into the wall, if possible. Heating by radiation through pipes placed in the floor is a trend that appears to be very acceptable.
- To discourage swimmers from spitting in the pool, cuspidors that are properly recessed into the wall should be provided.
- One or two tack boards should be located in the pool room. The surface should be made of cork, plastic, or similar material to permit easy tacking of posted material.
- The air temperature in the indoor pool area should be thermostatically controlled and maintained at approximately 5 degrees above the water temperature. The relative humidity should not exceed 70% for spectator comfort.

Maintenance

- Hot water outlets should be provided in the pool area in the number needed to enable maintenance personnel to clean decks.
- A room should be provided at a location immediately adjacent to the pool room for storage of instructional supplies, equipment, and cleaning gear. It is usually desirable to have a separate room for storage of cleaning equipment.
- There is a tendency to paint outdoor pools a light aqua blue color. This practice is not recommended. Pool basins should be white to produce the greatest degree of water clarity and visibility.

SIZE AND SHAPE OF POOLS

Great advances have been made from the traditional rectangular 60 by 30 foot pool that typified school pools in the 1920s and 1930s. Competitive swimming requirements, safety, and recreational needs have been the major factors influencing change in pool size and shape. Today's ideal design appears to be the multiple pool complex (Fig. 10-11), which provides separate facilities for diving, instruction/competition, and young children. The evolution of pool design has witnessed the L, T, and Z shapes, all of which attempt to provide for these specialized areas; however, the actual separation of pools by function as achieved by the multiple pool concept appears to be the best solution (Fig. 10-12). The cost is slightly higher, but the result is a safer and more manageable facility.

Motel, apartment, and residential pools, which are rarely concerned with meeting competition swimming requirements, increasingly favor the aesthetic appeal of free-form design.

On the other hand, practically all school, agency, college, and municipal pools are used for competition. Therefore they should have a regulation competitive course incorporated into their design. There are just two recognized competitive swimming courses in the United States, the 25-yard "short course," and the 50-meter "long course."

Recommended width of pools depends on the level of competition. For championship short-course meets, eight 7-foot lanes are recommended, whereas six lanes are adequate for dual competition. For long-course competition, eight 8-foot lanes are recommended. To assure that each lane is equal, a mini-

Fig. 10-11. Multiple-pool aquatic complex at the University School at Nova University in Florida.

Fig. 10-12. The Pennsylvania State University indoor three-pool complex. (Photo courtesy Pennsylvania State University Information Office.)

mum of 1½ feet between the outside lanes and the side wall should be provided.

The most desirable long-course pool in the United States is one that measures 50 meters in length and 25 yards in width, thus providing both an official long and short course. Competition can be held in any size pool, but it is best where possible to provide official courses. Pool planners should consult the AAU, NCAA, or Scholastic Swimming rule books as they begin their planning to determine whether any recent changes have been made in the rules.

CONSTRUCTION MATERIAL FOR IN-GROUND POOLS

Forty years ago practically every pool was constructed by using concrete. Since that time, many innovations in material and construction methods have appeared that have greatly reduced both the cost of pools and construction time. Materials now used include the following:

- Reinforced poured concrete
- Pneumatic concrete (often referred to as Gunite)
- Dry-pack concrete
- Steel
- Aluminum
- Fiberglass
- Vinyl liner

There have been some precast concrete pools constructed in Europe and a few made from brick and cement block.

Fig. 10-13. The pool at Cypress Gardens, Florida, under construction, showing the application of the plaster coat. (Photo courtesy General Portland Cement Co.)

The pool basin, whether made from poured concrete, Gunite, or the dry-pack method, usually has a finish coat covering its surface (Fig. 10-13). The most common types of finishes are as follows:

- Tile
- Plaster (marble dust)
- Epoxy
- Paint (rubber base)
- Neoprene rubber and hypalon

Some pools are finished initially by merely troweling the raw concrete to a smooth finish and delaying the placement of any other finish for four or five years. This practice is not recommended because algae and fungi have a strong affinity for rough surfaces.

TYPES OF FILTRATION

To maintain swimming pool water in a sanitary and safe state, the water must be circulated through filters. This is accomplished by the use of a pump. The rate of flow required by most health departments is a minimum of eight hours, with a six-hour rate preferred. Two typical systems are pressure diatomaceous earth and vacuum diatomaceous earth.

Types of filter media are as follows:

- Sand and gravel
- Diatomaceous earth
- Anthracite
- High-rate sand
- Cartridge

More filters use diatomaceous earth than any other medium. There are literally hundreds of different manufacturers of filters in this country. The essential thing to look for is whether they have been approved by the National Sanitary Foundation (NSF) and whether they conform to the requirements of local boards of health.

WATER TREATMENT AND CONTROL

Essential to swimming pools is clear water that is free of any harmful bacteria or virus forms. Filtration has much to do with keeping the water clear, but it does not sterilize water. This is the function of bactericides, the most common of which is chlorine.

Foreign substances are brought into the pool by swimmers and by wind. The latter represents a problem only for outdoor pools. Such foreign substances may contain harmful bacteria or viruses. Human carriers of such microorganisms may introduce them into a pool in a variety of ways. It is therefore essential that the sterilizing agent in the pool water be maintained in sufficient concentration (strength) to kill these harmful organisms almost instantaneously. It is inevitable at some time or other in the course of swimming around in a pool that a swimmer will ingest some water. This is why it is important that the water be free at all times from potentially harmful bacteria.

Chlorine in various forms, iodine, and bromine are the most commonly used chemicals to kill bacteria. They all belong to the chemical group called *halogens.*

The reader is referred to *Swimming Pool Operator's Guide* and *Swimming Pools—a Guide to their Planning, Design, and Operation,*[2,8] for a fuller discussion of the subject of water treatment.

Water temperature is important to the comfort of swimmers. A temperature of 80° F. is recommended for both competitive and recreational swimming. Air temperature in indoor pools should be around 85° F.

RECENT INNOVATIONS IN SWIMMING POOL DESIGN AND EQUIPMENT

Many innovations have occurred in the design and construction of pools since the end of World War II. Some of the most significant are described in this section.

Floating swimming pools. A pool that floats in lakes or rivers has recently been introduced. It employs a vinyl liner as the water container and uses the water that it floats in as the principal source of water (Fig. 10-14). The water is filtered before it is introduced into the pool. Additionally, portable pools that can be easily transported have enabled aquatic activities to be introduced into communities and schools where permanent facilities do not exist (Fig. 10-15).

Movable bulkheads. Although movable bulkheads have been around for some time, the hydraulic bulkhead that comes up from the floor is the most

Fig. 10-14. Model of a floating swimming pool construction. This pool is 200 feet in diameter with a center island. The vinyl liner serves as the water container. (Developed by Floating Pools, Inc.; Dan Duckham, architect, Fort Lauderdale, Florida; John Palmer Lutz, engineer, Fort Lauderdale, Florida.)

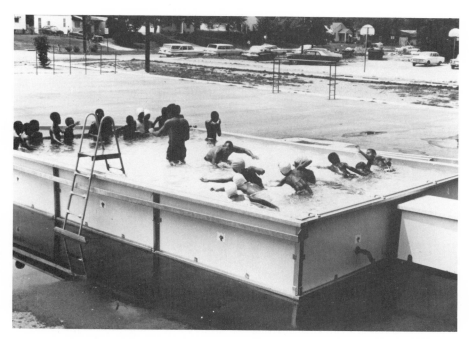

Fig. 10-15. Portable swimming pools, which can bring swimming facilities into virtually any community, are becoming more and more popular.

Fig. 10-16. Typical movable bulkhead for modifying pool lengths at University of Saskatchewan, Canada. It operates on runners that fit into roll-out gutter. (Photo courtesy Len Hillyard.)

Fig. 10-17. Movable bulkhead separates the diving area at the Michigan State University pool. (Photo courtesy Michigan State University Photographic Laboratory.)

recent to be introduced. Others that roll in the gutter or on the deck offer promise of inexpensive types of bulkheads. (See Figs. 10-16 and 10-17.)

Automation. Automation of pool operation (water circulation, chemical control, and temperature control) has finally been achieved. Such controllers provide for greater accuracy of water management, as well as a reduction in cost of manpower.

Continued.

Fig. 10-18. The pool at the Hommocks School in Mamaroneck, New York, is covered by an air-supported double pillow roof in the winter. In the summer the roof is rolled away, opening the pool to community use. (Photos courtesy Perkins & Will Partnership.)

Fig. 10-18, cont'd. For legend see p. 131.

Variable-depth bottoms. In Europe pool bottoms have been developed that may be raised and lowered hydraulically. This is excellent for accommodating young children in beginning classes.

Structures over pools. There have been many innovations in the types of structures used to create an indoor pool environment (Fig. 10-18). Some of the types are air structures, lightweight metal frame and fiberglass, geodesic dome, acrylic, conventionally designed building, removable building on railroad track, removable roof, and open sky dome with radiant people heaters. (See Figs. 10-19 to 10-21.)

Gutter design. The use of the word *gutter* is gradually being phased out. The modern term is *overflow systems*. Gutters were originally conceived as a means of skimming all floating debris, particularly sputum, from the pool and discharging it into the sewer. The pool water was circulated from bottom drains. Inlets were placed in the walls of pools. The recessed gutter, the first type of pool gutter developed, did afford a handhold for swimmers that was a good safety factor.

The first break from the recessed type of gutter was the roll-out type developed by the YMCA in the early 1930s. A modification of this design was introduced in 1936 by the Boys' Club of America. It was called the deck-level pool. Water comes over the pool wall onto the deck and goes into a shallow trench covered by a metal grate.

Fig. 10-19. Striking roof design of curved acrylic at the Echo Park Pools, Hempstead, New York, contributes to the interior esthetics of the facility.

Both of these systems have a serious defect in that they are unable to provide for the "surge" of water resulting from the displacement of water by swimmers. Subsequently, in the early 1940s the Boys' Clubs modified their original design, which had a "balancing tank" in the filter room to provide for the surge water, to include a deep trench in the deck 18 inches wide and from 2 to 8 feet deep.

Fig. 10-20. Swimming pool structure at Ball State University, Muncie, Indiana. (Photo by Rex Miller.)

Fig. 10-21. Exciting architectural design of the Tokyo Olympic Pool.

This worked fairly well, but the trench cover as designed was incapable of handling the surge capacity as quickly as desired. Subsequently, in the late 1950s an improved cover was designed that had the ability to accommodate almost instantly all water going over the pool wall. This system is now known as the *rimflow system* (Fig. 10-22).

Fig. 10-22. Example of the rimflow system of water circulation.

Fig. 10-23. Carpeting for pool decks, such as at this installation at Decatur, Alabama, is becoming more popular. (Deering Milliken's Foresight Carpeting by Monsanto.)

Solar heating. The use of solar energy to heat swimming water and even homes and schools has been successfully accomplished in a number of places. Los Angeles County has conducted tests on scale models of twelve different types of solar heat collectors for probable use in that country's public pools.

With the energy crisis a matter of worldwide concern, solar energy will be looked at critically as one of the solutions to heating pools and natatoriums in this country as well as in others.

Carpeting of pool decks. School corridors and locker rooms have been successfully carpeted, and now pool planners are beginning to look toward carpeting for pool decks. Several companies have been experimenting with carpeting (Fig. 10-23).

Following are essential characteristics that all pool carpets must possess. They must:

- Be able to be sterilized to keep them free of bacteria
- Be fungi and algae free, or at least be able to be cleaned to eliminate these undesirable organisms when they appear
- Have a life of at least five years
- Be easily removed so that the deck underneath can be cleaned
- Be nonslip when wet
- Be available in a variety of colors

Prefabrication of pool tanks. The most successful system of prefabrication of pool walls, bottoms, and decks has been achieved in Germany. Pool floors are built of prefabricated concrete slabs laid on precast concrete girders.

Fig. 10-24. Typical indoor therapeutic pool, Kings Point, Delray Beach, Florida. (Photo courtesy United Pools, Fort Lauderdale, Florida.)

Walls are constructed of large prebuilt sections, complete with interior finishes and overflow rims. The system has not caught on in this country because of the high cost of shipping and handling the large slabs. Nevertheless, it is expected that this method of pool construction will become more popular in the future.

Therapeutic pools, or "spas" (Fig. 10-24). Pools designed to have therapeutic value, often referred to as "spa" pools, have gained in popularity in this country, particularly with homeowners. A major feature of these pools is the jet spray, which forces a strong stream of water into the pool. One or more of such jet heads are located in the wall of the pool and cause the water to circulate rapidly around the pool. The other major feature of these pools is the water temperature, which is usually kept between 100° and 110° F.

An increasing number of communities and schools are including such pools as a part of their aquatic complexes. Older people are particularly attracted to these pools, some seeking to gain relief from aches and pains often brought on by an arthritic condition. School and community pools frequently are built with ramps and other aids for handicapped users (Fig. 10-25).

Safety pads for pool bottoms. As a means of reducing injuries resulting from hitting the bottom of the pool, Nova University in Fort Lauderdale, Florida, is experimenting with safety cushions made of closed cellular material. Under diving boards the safety pad is an inch thick, and on the bottom of children's pools the pad is ¼ inch thick.

Wave pools. The advent of surfing as a popular recreational activity, as well as the increase in instruction in canoeing and boating that frequently requires

Fig. 10-25. Ramps leading into pool facilitate the management of wheelchairs.

137

Fig. 10-26. Surfing conditions, including waves and lush foliage, are now found indoors, as well as at the beachfront. (Photos courtesy Japan National Tourist Organization.)

some natural wave conditions, has created a need for pools that can simulate these conditions. Two fine examples of pools of this type are located in Tempe, Arizona, and just outside Tokyo, Japan (Fig. 10-26).

SAFETY

Safety in and around swimming pools is the responsibility of everyone related to the pool, including the users.

Safety responsibility begins when the pool is in the conceptual stage. Involved in this process is the owner, the designer, the builder, the person who maintains the facility, manufacturers of pool equipment, the pool manager, instructors, lifeguards, and others who might have a role in the total design construction operation process.

Each can be held accountable for integrating safety principles and practices into each facet of the overall function of the pool. For the architect or designer this means adherence to all applicable safety and health codes and standards; for the builder, rigid attention to materials, requirements, and quality control; and from an operational point of view, the employment of only professionally qualified personnel.

Equipment and pool manufacturers have a particular responsibility to determine that (1) their products are safely designed, (2) instructions for their installation and use are explicit, and (3) warnings about misuse are of the required intensity.

Within institutional facilities accident-free operation is a management responsibility. Certain authority and specific duties may be delegated to supervisors, lifeguards, instructors, and maintenance personnel, but the pool manager or operating head is the person who is ultimately responsible for the safe operation of the pool.

REFERENCES

1. Data and reference annual, 1972, 1973, Hoffman Publications, Inc., P. O. Box 11299, 3000 N.E. 30th Place, Fort Lauderdale, Fla. 33306.
2. Gabrielsen, Milton A., editor: Swimming pools—a guide to their planning, design and operation, Council for National Cooperation in Aquatics, Fort Lauderdale, Fla., 1974, Hoffman Publications, Inc.
3. Guide for planning facilities for athletics, recreation, physical and health education, Chicago, 1965, The Athletic Institute, Inc., Merchandise Mart.
4. Suggested minimum standards for public swimming pools, 1969, National Swimming Pool Institute, 2000 "K" Street, N.W., Washington, D.C. 20006.
5. Suggested ordinance and regulations covering public swimming pools, New York, 1964, The American Public Health Association.
6. Swimming pool market report, Fort Lauderdale, Fla., Hoffman Publications, Inc.
7. Swimming Pool Weekly and Swimming Pool Age, Fort Lauderdale, Fla., Hoffman Publications, Inc.
8. Thomas, Dave: Swimming pool operator's guide, Washington, D.C., 1972, National Swimming Pool Institute.

CHAPTER 11

Ice facilities

James Fullerton*

GROWTH OF ICE SKATING IN THE UNITED STATES

Skating dates as far back as the Greek and Roman Empires. It became popular in Scandinavia about 3000 years ago. The skates were primitive, and the blades were first made of wood.

The early English settlers in Canada and the United States reportedly brought the sport to the North American continent, although many historians claim the American Indians of Canada played hockey in the winter as a substitute for lacrosse. By the late 1800s hockey was played in Canada. Shortly thereafter, colleges in the northern United States began to play. In 1892 the first intercollegiate hockey game in the United States was played between Harvard University and Brown University in Boston. Both hockey and figure skating were features of the 1924 Olympics at Chamonix in France. In 1932, Sonja Henie, an Olympic skater from Norway, popularized free skating in her many appearances all over the world. (See Fig. 11-1.)

Ice shows further popularized free skating, especially through films and later through television. Today there are well over 800 artificial ice auditoriums in the United States in all parts of the country. The advent of pneumatic structures and other reasonably economical building shell technologies has enabled ice activities to take place all year round in practically every geographical location and not to be limited to a cold-weather climate (Fig. 11-2). Today ice arenas are open year-round to accommodate figure skating and hockey patrons. The summer months find hundreds of well-qualified instructors conducting classes in skating and hockey that are as profitable as they are popular. Summer ice hockey camps for children are proliferating throughout the country. The growth and popularity of professional ice hockey in the United States, with the "star" status afforded many of its key performers, has been a major factor in this skating boom. The national recreation explosion and the international television coverage given to figure skating championships have similarly contributed significantly to the demand for more ice rink facilities.

ICE ARENAS

A rectangular building arena is less expensive to construct. However, if seating is desired, a circular rink seems preferable. The roof construction is

---

* For many years varsity hockey coach at Brown University and coach of the United States National Collegiate hockey team, Mr. Fullerton is presently on the staff of the New York Islanders of the National Hockey League.

Fig. 11-1. The figure skating, hockey, and recreational skating boom has resulted in the proliferation of ice arenas all over the country.

Fig. 11-2. Typical air structure for an ice rink.

Fig. 11-3. The beautiful Wesleyan University Hockey Rink in Middletown, Connecticut, where the rink enclosure is demountable so that the space can be used for large nonskating activities such as graduations and concerts. (Photos courtesy Warner Burns Toan Lunde, architects; Louis Reens, photographer.)

expensive in either case because of the span necessary to cover an ice area 85 by 200 feet. Building codes in an area dictate parameters for planning and construction. For example, emergency machinery has to be installed in case of power failure—the codes demand this expense. Space for parking cars should be at the ratio of one car space for every three seats. The parking cost must be considered as part of the building cost. All safety codes are paramount and, of course, must be adhered to. (See Fig. 11-3.)

If land space is not a problem, a one-story building with cells projecting will give an excellent, practical, and functional edifice. If space is a problem, a multifloor building should be considered, with two or three floors above the

Fig. 11-3, cont'd. For legend see opposite page.

auditorium part of the building. Low ceilings should be avoided because some of the essential machinery is gasoline driven, and sufficient oxygen must be available. Today it is possible to measure the carbon monoxide and dioxide percentages and use warning systems. Acoustics appear to be better for teaching and coaching when higher ceilings are used.

SCHEDULED USE OF THE ARENA

The prime function of any arena is to provide recreational facilities for students and the community, as well as to accommodate intramural skating and hockey. Rentals at a nominal fee are customary in most arenas, providing the rentals do not encroach unreasonably on recreational needs. It is imperative that those charged with the responsibility of the program realize the cost of operating an ice arena, especially in times of financial belt tightening and budget limitations. Ice sports are not cheap; any funds brought into the building should be used for maintenance and operation, especially the income over and beyond gate receipts for scheduled events.

During seasons when ice is out of the arena, an efficient management will schedule events such as speakers, musical groups, symposiums, dances, and circuses.

Fig. 11-4. Tennis over the ice at the Boston Garden.

Fig. 11-5. Portable basketball court on the ice arena at the Hippodrome Auditorium, Waterloo, Iowa. (Photo courtesy Championship Sports Floors, Inc.)

Fig. 11-6. Children skate on an experimental synthetic ice surface in the West Suburban YMCA in Chicago, Illinois.

One must realize that events other than ice spectaculars can be scheduled with the ice on the floor. Synthetic coverings or wooden flooring can be used efficiently, and the transition will require only three or four hours, depending on the labor available. This is a common practice, particularly in professional sports arenas where wooden basketball courts are frequently placed on top of the ice rink. (See Figs. 11-4 and 11-5.)

Experimentation is underway to develop a synthetic skating surface (Fig. 11-6), and although this technology has not as yet been adequately developed to make it feasible to replace ice, we can look forward to the day when this will be a common and economical replacement for what we now know as ice.

INSTALLATION CONSIDERATIONS FOR YEAR-ROUND USE

All ice rinks built for school or community programs should be built for year-round utilization. Community ice rinks must be insulated for 80° to 120° F. outside temperatures. Air conditioning and dehumidification are paramount factors in construction. Refrigeration plants can absorb the chilling effect in summer as well as removal of moisture in the air. Moisture and condensation of moisture have a deleterious effect on the building and ice surface. A negative safety factor exists, too, in that condensed moisture means slippery surfaces. Fog erodes the ice surface.

LIGHTING AND ACOUSTICS

A major consideration in lighting for any ice arena is the ability to accommodate color television transmission. There must be sufficient candlepower to do this, and although the ice is colored to dull the light reflection, there are other events that need strong lighting.

Girders, walls, uncoated ceilings, etc. have to be treated for sound effects. Hockey and other sports are often noisy, and sound has to be controlled by excellent acoustical effects. This is especially true for public address systems, music, and oratory.

SEATING

Many ice arenas or auditoriums are designed to accommodate many disparate functions that produce income, as well as satisfying the needs of various institutional functions. Therefore it is recommended that comfortable seats be installed. The number of seats per aisle and width and the number of individual seats are determined by the local building code. Ingress and egress to seating areas from within as well as outside the building is also controlled by the building code. Both outside and inside aisles and seating conformations must consider the needs of the handicapped population.

REFRIGERATION PLANT

Sufficient tonnage of refrigeration is necessary for year-round use, and it is recommended that the auditorium be kept around 68° to 70° F. during the winter months. A temperature of 50° to 60° F. is ideal for hockey practice, figure skating, or general skating. There must be at least two compressors to remove the heat from the liquid used in the miles of pipes. An auxiliary compressor is advised, and the three can be alternated or run at a lower speed. In addition, there must be at least two pumps that force the liquid through the pipes. One is a reserve. Ammonia or Freon gas is generally used in the compressors. Some municipal codes insist on Freon because it is not explosive. Ice surfaces are recommended to be 200 by 85 feet, which requires about ten miles of pipe to refrigerate the area. The pipes are embedded in concrete of sufficient strength to withstand heavy floor loads for circuses, boxing, basketball, and automobile shows and artificial floor coverings for tennis, rodeos, horse shows, and track meets.

The pipes are usually set on sand, under which is gravel on synthetic insulation to ensure that the "cold" goes up into the concrete and is not lost in the subsurface.

After the ice is made, the refrigerant in the pipes is kept between 14° and 25°F. The lower temperature is generally used when there are many spectators in the auditorium and management wishes to keep a 70° F. auditorium temperature. A lower temperature is required in summer months.

As in all mechanical units, there are readings to take to ensure efficiency, but in addition, there are master boards that monitor the proper functioning of each unit. If for any reason a unit malfunctions, a warning light appears and trips an alarm warning the engineers. If the malfunction should occur during the night when there might not be engineer coverage, this alarm should be connected to a telephone switchboard. A six- or eight-hour shutdown can destroy an ice surface.

ICE MAKING

The cement floor on which the ice surface rests has to be at a temperature below freezing. Naturally when water is sprayed on the surface, the heat must be removed before the water freezes, so it is desirable to go to a brine temperature below 18° F. "Brine" is the liquid circulated through the ten miles of pipes.

The concrete floor should be clean of all foreign matter. Then the water is sprayed on. Generally tap water is around 50° F. The spray hoses go from one end to the other; after about ¼ inch of ice is made, the ice surface is sprayed with a colored water paint. This paint dries in a short time, and more water spraying is repeated until another ¼ inch of ice is made. After the ¼ inch is reached, it is recommended that an ice resurfacing machine be used for flooding.

An ice resurfacing machine is an absolute essential in any arena. The machine actually does at least three jobs: (1) plane the ice, (2) pick up the shavings made by planing or skating, and (3) put a coat of either warm or cold water on the surface. The three steps can be done in one operation or individually. If the ice were not painted, it would be dark in color, and it would be difficult to see the hockey puck or skating figures. About ½ inch of ice is sufficient for a safe program. A little more depth of thickness is desirable for beginning figure skaters who are jumping or for those persons in the early training periods for hockey. Many hockey games are actually played on ⅜ inch of ice. Once the ice is made, a "brine" temperature of 22° F. is usually sufficient for a building kept at 50° to 55° F.

Removal of ice can be done in several ways: (1) continual planing to a depth of about ⅛ inch and then applying hot water; (2) raising the brine temperature and breaking the bond between ice and concrete floor; and (3) spraying hot water until the ice has melted. The melted ice water can be "sucked up" by the surfacing machine, or it can be pushed out of the rink into "scuppers" (drains) by large squeegees. In any case, the brine temperature must be raised. Caution must be used in removing the layer of painted ice.

SIDE (DASHER) BOARDS AND KICK BOARDS

There are usually two sets of boards enclosing the ice surface. One set is referred to as the side boards (dasher boards), which separate the ice from the audience. The second set is the kick boards, preferably oak, usually 8 to 10 inches high, which act as buffer shields for skate blades. The side boards vary in height from 45 to 50 inches and are made of a synthetic material that is stronger than wood or plywood.

On top of the side boards a Plexiglas or similar nonshatterable glass is attached. This is obviously a safety measure to protect both skaters and spectators. A steel mesh fencing is less expensive than Plexiglas.

PENALTY BOX AND TIMER'S BOX FOR HOCKEY

The timer's box is situated between the players' penalty boxes and on the opposite side of the rink from the players' box. The timer's box has room for three people, whereas the players' penalty box should accommodate at least four players plus an attendant. The doors to the penalty box and the players' box should open inward, and the doors of each should be more toward the goal than the center of the rink. It is not necessary to have nonbreakable glass or wire fencing in front of the penalty box or players' box, but it is a necessity in front of the timer's box.

PLAYERS' BOXES

Each hockey team is allowed a maximum of eighteen players to dress for each game. For example, the rules for college hockey state that a manager, coach, and trainer, or not more than three nonplayer personnel, may be on each bench. This means at least twenty-one people could be on the bench, but six are playing at one time, so a minimum of fifteen seats are necessary. Both players' benches should be on one side of the rink. The players' boxes should be separated by a few feet. They should be surrounded by wire fencing or preferably nonbreakable glass to protect players and spectators alike.

The center of the players' box should be lower than the front and back, allowing the "snow" or moisture melting from the skates to flow into a drain and alleviate housekeeping problems. Any areas where skaters walk should have an all-weather matting or suitable substitute.

It is suggested that a coach's "walk area" be available behind the players' bench or benches.

THE CLOCK

A four-face clock scoreboard hanging over midice is preferable in any hockey arena in which large numbers of spectators are accommodated. A clock scoreboard at both ends or one end is a second choice. The scoreboard should give the score, penalty numbers, and time of each penalty, plus the time left to play in each period and an indicator as to the period of the game.

ICE RESURFACING MACHINE

An ice resurfacing machine costs over $10,000 and does the work of several adults in a very short time. This machine, in making ice, accomplishes three jobs. (1) It planes the ice surface with a steel blade very similar to the knife used to cut newsprint. This blade is sharpened frequently, and at least two sharp spares should be on hand. (2) A wormgear attached to an endless belt with rubber paddles picks up the "snow" or scrapings caused by skating and planing and deposits it in the machine. (3) A layer of warm water is spread evenly at the rear of the machine to the width of the machine. A light or heavy spread of water can be applied. The entrance to the rink is usually at one end of the rink through gates in the side boards. The machine drives to a special area where it can dump the "snow," or the "snow" can be melted in the machine by use of hot water or steam. The ice resurfacing machine can also vacuum excess water off the concrete slab.

LOCKER ROOMS

There should be an adequate number of locker rooms in the facility to accommodate the proposed program. One large locker room should have an adjacent equipment room plus shower heads, urinals, and toilets. A second room should have ingress and egress to the shower and toilet facilities. Equal facilities should be built for men and women. A varsity team room should have adequate, well-aired open locker space with sufficient hooks and space for basic training needs, as well as a trainer's table. Other rooms to consider include four good-sized rooms for visiting teams, intramural teams, youth hockey teams, skate changing, and faculty or graduate activities. Showers and toilets should be accessible to each room. There is no need for lockers in a room used by visiting teams. However, training tables and blackboards should be available.

LAUNDRY ROOM

If the ice slab is in a structure separate from the other recreation facilities, a laundry room should be available to wash and dry equipment. The laundry service should be available to all skaters.

SKATE SHARPENING ROOM

A skate sharpening room, easily accessible to all patrons, should be on the ice level area. The room should have sufficient and adequate storage bins to hold individual pairs of skates. This room is particularly essential when the rink is open for community use.

The sharpening machinery should be top grade and able to sharpen hockey and figure skates with all the necessary accoutrements. All safety rules set up by the rink manager must be adhered to. Fees for sharpening should be nominal, and the sharpener should be reimbursed from these fees. It is customary for a sharpener to be employed by the rink manager in a custodial or equipment category. Customarily there is no charge for the recognized varsity, junior varsity, or freshmen teams of either sex. This policy should be set by mutual consent of those in charge of programming for the rink.

CUSTODIAL PERSONNEL

The coordination of custodial duties with ice making is of paramount importance. The staff must receive special training in ice techniques. After games or rentals attended by large crowds the facility should be cleaned.

Regular custodians can be trained as ice machine operators, so that there is always a training program in force. Generally the rinks are open from early morning to midnight for rentals or use. One trained ice man and three custodians comprise a normal working shift. In addition, there must be an engineer. Municipal codes dictate the safety rules for mechanical equipment.

For reasons of safety, new ice is usually made every hour except for games, when new ice is made at the end of each period. It is possible to go two hours before making new ice during public skating, but it is not recommended. There should be at least ½ inch of ice in thickness. Figure skating and patch skating demand new ice.

PUBLIC ROOMS AND CONCESSIONS

Public rooms for scheduled events should be made available on the level above the ice to keep all nonparticipants away from the performers. Concessions should also be conveniently and efficiently situated above ice level.

For public skating, rental groups, or general skating, the rooms should be made available. Dressing rooms are not necessary for general skating. Hooks and benches are installed near ingress and egress areas as provided by local municipal codes.

CHAPTER 12

On the drawing board

For college students particularly, this should be the most enjoyable chapter in this book. For if it is true that the young can luxuriate in the process of dreaming about the future, this chapter will offer subject matter for dreams of physical education and recreation facilities. We will explore some of the dreams of current planners, architects, and facility managers, who are attempting to project some innovative thinking into the form and substance of operating facilities for sports and recreation.

Some of the projects we will report on are already on architects' drawing boards, some are in advanced stages of planning, and some are operational in experimental programs. Others are merely concepts and untested ideas that are still locked into the thoughts of those who think about sports and recreation for the future. But these are the thoughts that ought to be "kicked around" in class and subjected to the scrutiny, enthusiasm, and probing appraisal that the college community is best qualified to offer. These are the thoughts and dreams of which progress is made.

It was relatively few years ago that synthetic surfaces and air bubbles could have been similarly categorized, and in just a few years they substantially changed the sports and recreation habits of the world. Are there any latent revolutionary possibilities lurking in some of these newer "on the drawing board" ideas? Do not outlaw the possibility of an air roof, a roof composed of air blasts that meet and form a volcanic cone over the open area (Fig. 12-1).

Our inclusion of these examples in this chapter is in no way intended to serve as an endorsement of the concepts or products. Rather, it is intended to offer students, teachers, and architects a basis for further examination of the state of the art of physical education and sports facilities. However, the inclusion of these examples is evidence, in itself, that our interest and curiosity has been stimulated by the possibilities inherent in them.

FITNESS CORNERS IN ELEMENTARY SCHOOLS

If physical fitness is a major goal of school programs of physical education, shouldn't the school plant itself provide some opportunity for physical activity, aside from the gymnasium, for which children are routinely scheduled?

Consider the following, a discussion of which first appeared in *The Journal for Health, Physical Education and Recreation:*

School buildings are usually designed to move kids from place to place quickly and without unnecessary steps. Maybe this is all wrong. Maybe school should provide for a vigorous five minute walk between classes or to and from different places within the school. Perhaps inclines and spirals would require the expenditure of some energy.

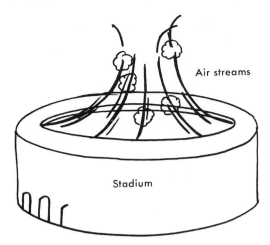

Air streams

Stadium

Fig. 12-1. The air roof, produced by continuous jets of air meeting above the center of a playing area, forms a protective ceiling that turns the elements aside. The need for a membrane roof, tensile or pneumatic, is eliminated.

Maybe elementary schools should have places to run and to jump in each classroom, or adjacent to each classroom. With soundproofing now possible in every school, maybe the corridors should become indoor tracks and play areas.

Schools should be built with some built-in physical challenge for young people. Pathways can be designed which require a child to jump over a brook, to swing across a gulley, to climb a wall—for those who want to. Couldn't there be alternative ways to move about a school—an easy way and a hard way—the hard way requiring some dexterity or strength or exertion?

The child's school environment should not scream "don't do it" at him. Rather, it should subtly say "try it." Let's spread the physical education period throughout the day: between periods, during periods, walking to the bus, enroute to lunch, returning from the bathroom. This can be done by spreading his gym all over the school grounds, into the classrooms and corridors.

A gym all over the school site? Why not? Chinning bars in the halls—jumping mats in the corridors—real climbable walls around the perimeter of the grounds—live trees to swing from—natural hills or man-made inclines to walk—walls to throw a ball against —a roof to run around—a carpeted corridor for stunts or tumbling—a classroom that says "move around"—some stand-up desks to work at—stationary bicycles in rooms— rowing machines—a place to live out for the weekend—an outdoor exploration area. But most of all, an educational philosophy that encourages youngsters to make use of these things, and to do things.

Elementary classrooms have science corners and library corners and other specialized study areas. Why not a fitness corner in each classroom? Specifically, I'm talking about *physical education carrels* (physi-carrel education, if you will) operating on an individual basis for learning, just as other study carrels are. Why not mini-gyms in every classroom? Now, just as a child goes to the library corner for reference or study materials, he can similarly take three or four minutes from time to time and utilize the exercise and fitness equipment in the fitness carrel or fitness corner of his room. It could become as easy and accepted as the individual work that goes on at the other individual study areas.*

---

*From Ezersky, Eugene M.: Mini-gyms and fitness corners, The Journal For Health, Physical Education and Recreation 43:38-39, Jan., 1972.

Further rationale and support for this concept comes from Irwin Tobin, Director of Health and Physical Education for the New York City Public Schools. In a memo to school supervisors, reported in a national professional newsletter, Tobin states the following:

What really helps children learn may be the example that adults set for students. Youngsters are very perceptive and soon understand priorities by the actions of their parents and teachers. It is soon clear that reading is a major desirable goal by the amount of time spent in teaching reading and by the kinds of materials made available in the "Reading Corner." Science is shown to be an important part of the school's activities by the expensive equipment that is provided for the "Science Corner." Students are impressed by the variety of materials available to teaching math in the "Math Corner." I suspect that students get another kind of message when they see little time devoted to health and physical fitness and have no opportunity in the classroom for fitness activities. Accordingly, if we provide a "Physical Fitness Corner" in classrooms, the message of priorities will soon become clear to the pupils.*

In essence, then, fitness corners are recommended because of their value in the development of fitness in school youth, as well as for their contribution to a positive image for physical education.

LARGE ACREAGE ROOFTOP PARKS

Rooftop recreation is rather commonplace throughout the world. We have become accustomed to seeing tennis played on the roof of a parking garage or swimming pools on the roofs of high-rise apartment buildings. However, consider the possibilities of developing a rooftop recreation complex on thirty acres. The New York State Parks and Recreation Commission is.

Riverbank State Park, in the heart of Manhattan, will be the most ambitious rooftop recreation development ever undertaken. It will be constructed on top of the North River Pollution Control Plant, a sewerage treatment facility; it will consist of thirty acres, eight city blocks long, extending 600 to 800 feet out over the Hudson River. The roof deck will be 60 to 75 feet above the river with access bridges from several points along the shore. Among the facilities to be included in this complex are play fields, basketball and tennis courts, swimming pools, and bicycle and pedestrian paths. A restaurant and snack bar will be set in grassy landscaped areas. (See Fig. 12-2.)

The completion of this project must await construction of the plant; thus it may take many years. Additionally, the magnitude of the undertaking coupled with the complicated problems involved in building over water suggests that this will be an expensive project and will require further modifications of preliminary plans. Nevertheless, with available urban land space becoming more and more scarce as Americans move further and further toward an urban-centered society, the prospect of large-scale recreation areas atop other city buildings becomes more and more attractive.

*From Klappholz, Lowell A.: The physical education newsletter, Old Saybrook, Conn., April 1, 1975, Physical Education Publications.

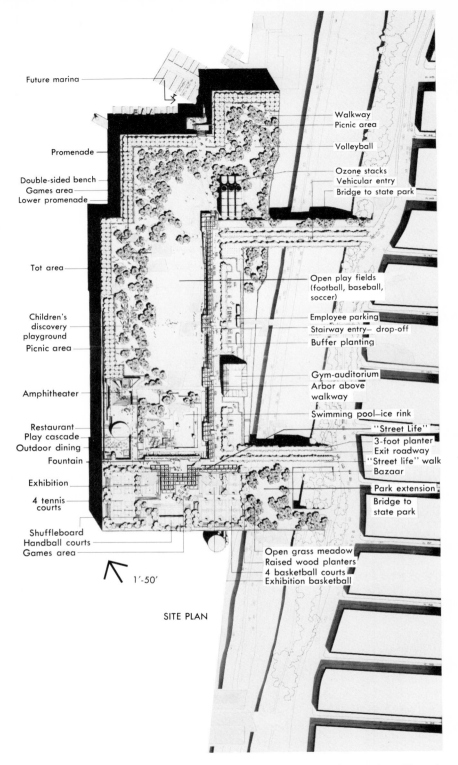

Future marina

Walkway
Picnic area

Promenade

Volleyball

Double-sided bench
Games area
Lower promenade

Ozone stacks
Vehicular entry
Bridge to state park

Tot area

Open play fields
(football, baseball,
soccer)

Children's
discovery
playground
Picnic area

Employee parking
Stairway entry— drop-off
Buffer planting

Amphitheater

Gym-auditorium
Arbor above
walkway
Swimming pool—ice rink

Restaurant
Play cascade
Outdoor dining

"Street Life"
3-foot planter
Exit roadway
"Street life" walk
Bazaar

Fountain

Exhibition

4 tennis
courts

Park extension
Bridge to
state park

Shuffleboard
Handball courts
Games area

1'-50'

Open grass meadow
Raised wood planters
4 basketball courts
Exhibition basketball

SITE PLAN

Fig. 12-2. Riverbank State Park, planned to be built atop the Hudson River in New York City. (Courtesy Bond Ryder Associates, Lawrence Halprin Associates, and New York State Parks Commission.)

154

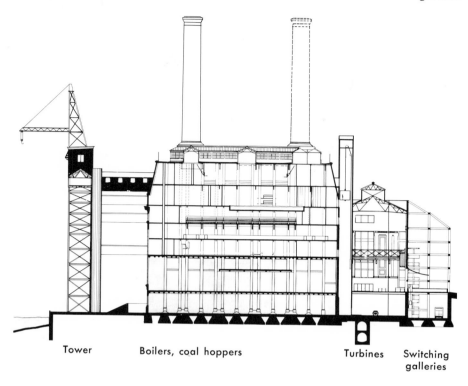

Tower   Boilers, coal hoppers   Turbines   Switching
                                                                      galleries

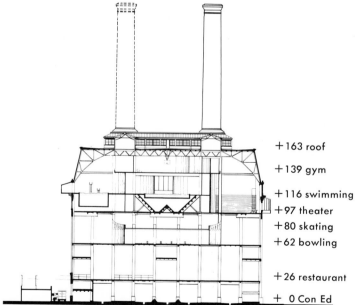

+163 roof
+139 gym
+116 swimming
+97 theater
+80 skating
+62 bowling

+26 restaurant

+ 0 Con Ed

Fig. 12-3. Proposed activities building for Sherman Creek State Park utilizes a 70-year-old Con Edison generating station. (Courtesy Richard Dattner & Associates, architects.)

The detailed and serious preliminary planning on the part of so prestigious a recreation agency as the New York State Park and Recreation Commission adds significant stature to this concept for our recreation resources in the future.

CONVERSIONS TO LEISURE CENTERS

Another fascinating proposed project of the New York State Park and Recreation Commission has to do with the conversion of a phased-out Con Edison generating plant to a multiuse activity building at the heart of a forty-acre recreational complex (Fig. 12-3). This activities building would provide interior spaces not otherwise available at a significant cost saving because of the reuse of the existing foundations, structure, and enclosure. This building, built in 1908, has high ceilings and huge open spaces that lends it very well to recreational use.

Tentative plans for the Sherman Creek State Park call for eight levels housing facilities for a marina, bowling, skating, swimming, gymnasium, restaurants, and gallery areas. Both of these innovative facilities propose to serve high-density population areas of New York City. As with the aforementioned Riverbank project, this is still very much in the planning stage, and no doubt some serious hurdles lie ahead. The plans for the conversion of the building, however, are fascinating and could well serve as a model for approaching similar conversions of other large buildings with wide and high open spaces.*

The United States is now experiencing a phenomenon hitherto unknown to educators: the closing of elementary schools because of a decrease in school-age children and shifting demographical factors. What do you think of the idea of converting these vacated buildings to sports and recreation facilities for *all* in the community? Fees, rentals, and occupancy by other governmental agencies can substantially reduce the financial burden imposed by these school vacancies.

INDOOR FACILITIES FOR OUTDOOR SKILLS

Recreation and sports facilities for the 1970s and 1980s will undoubtedly be found more and more in the wide open spaces of parkland and forests. Recreation is moving outward into the natural environment to accommodate such activities as hiking, orienteering, mountaineering, rock climbing, camping, and cross-country skiing. Recreation planners and administrators can no longer look only to the traditional gymnasiums, playgrounds, and recreation centers for their facilities, but must now turn as well to the mountains, streams, forests, and lakes. Environmental and conservation considerations will become an important component in educating youngsters about recreation in natural outdoor settings.

---

*Information about Sherman Creek State Park and the Riverbank Project can be obtained by writing the State Park and Recreation Commission for the City of New York, 1700 Broadway, New York, N.Y. 10019.

Similarly, other factors in the recreation education process have suddenly loomed up as worthy of serious examination. How do city children, for example, get experience and training in such skills as backpacking, campsite management, rock and mountain climbing, and compass orientation when their environment generally does not have the elements to teach these. It is not uncommon for city children to be taken on a school camping trip for three or four days, where very basic skills can be crammed into a crash course. However, contrast this to the amount of time spent on teaching baseball, basketball, and tennis when local school facilities can be used. Additionally, these outdoor living activities happen initially in a setting that is foreign and consequently frightening to most urban-oriented people, forest and mountain wilderness. Is there a way to bring this training for the outdoors indoors?

The Portledge School, a private coeducational day school in Locust Valley, New York, has developed a "climbing wall" in the gymnasium that has become

Fig. 12-4. The Climbing Wall at the Portledge School in Locust Valley, New York, simulates rock climbing experiences. (Photo by Peter Ezersky.)

an exciting and educationally sound addition to their school program. Here boys and girls in the intermediate and senior schools are taught the techniques of rock climbing, while at the same time they develop self-confidence and an understanding of the essential elements of cooperation. They learn about working together in an atmosphere of mutual trust, with one guiding and protecting the other through various rock climbing simulations. They are taught safety regulations and the essential knots for climbing, belaying, and repelling. This 40-foot high brick wall is replete with ledges, handholds, and a chimney climb, and it is designed to provide challenging experiences for elementary climbing right up through more difficult tasks. (See Fig. 12-4.)

The teachers at this facility are all trained and certified by Outward Bound, Inc., or other accredited climbing schools, and parental consent is required. Constant upgrading of technique and refresher courses are provided for the teachers. It has proved to be a very popular activity, particularly for those youngsters who might not normally excel in the traditional eye-hand-ball coordination skills of American sports, where the stress is on team competition. Rather, it is a "solo" challenge in which youngsters achieve a considerable sense of achievement as they learn to conquer the wall and themselves.

Fig. 12-5. Synthetic ice is in its experimental phase, such as this installation at the West Suburban YMCA in Chicago, Illinois.

SYNTHETIC ICE (Fig. 12-5)

Experimentation is underway to develop a synthetic skating surface that will permit skating without ice. A plastic surface that can be installed like floor tiles or linoleum is currently being tested. Although this technology has not as yet been fully developed, we can look forward to the day when this will be a common and economical replacement for ice. Skating on a synthetic surface is a little "slower" than on ice, so its main value may be in training rinks, not to replace ice, but rather as a supplement that is expected to cost about half what a traditional artificial ice system does.

TURNTABLE ATHLETIC FACILITIES (Fig. 12-6)

A recent development in auditorium design holds promise for accommodating spectator seats or athletic facilities for sports events. This development, using the Macton divisible auditorium turntable system, enables a school to divide a large space into small spaces by installing some of the seating on turntables. A wall is installed at the rear of the turntables containing rows of auditorium seats. When the turntables face front, the seats are part of the auditorium; when they are reversed, the walls separate the seats into self-contained classrooms.

The implications for sports facilities in this concept are particularly important. Since spectator seating is so expensive a part of athletic facility construction costs, shared seating that can be used at two or three courts or arenas represents a considerable cost and space saving. By using shared seats in the middle of regularly built courts and arenas, a major spectator event can be staged at the same time that regular intramural or school service courses are underway in adjacent facilities.

Several combinations of uses become apparent when the turntable concept is adopted. For example, a large auditorium-like space can be divided to provide a large lecture hall, smaller lecture rooms, and laboratories. A large gym space can be separated into a weight room, a wrestling or combatives station, or a gymnastics practice station. The interesting aspect of the turntable concept is that it has application for institutions with large space needs as well as for those places which need multiple facilities in a limited space.

INDIVIDUALIZED BOUNDARY MARKERS

The converging lines of different colors and widths that crisscross gymnasium floors are something that the sports spectator and participant has long taken as a necessary fact of competitive life. This, however, will be changing as court marking procedures become more sophisticated. Floor markings built into the floor surface and illuminated specifically for each game are at advanced planning stages under test conditions. So, when the basketball game is underway, only the basketball markings show, avoiding confusion on the part of officials, players, and spectators. Electrical or other energy impulses similarly can play an important part in determing whether a ball "hit the line" or

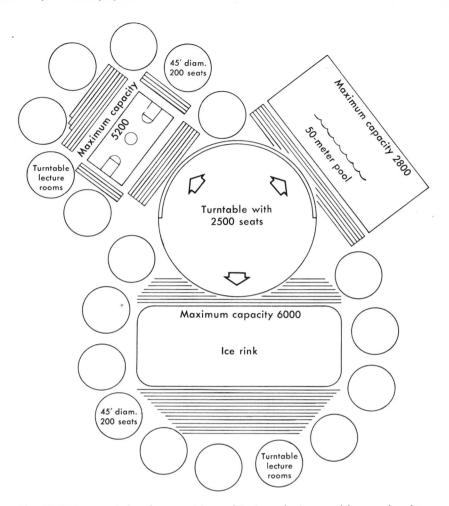

Fig. 12-6. A recent development in auditorium design enables a school to divide a large space into small spaces by installing some of the seating on turntables. A wall is installed at the rear of the turntables containing rows of auditorium seats. When the turntables face front, the seats are part of the auditorium; when they are reversed, the walls separate the seats into self-contained classrooms. Designers have proposed adapting the same principle to physical recreation facilities so that the turntables provide classrooms or grandstands.

not, which might provide some breakthrough in "close call" officiating techniques.

PREPARATION FOR THE METRIC SYSTEM

The metric system of measurement is upon us. Any new or converted facility *must* be planned to accommodate new metric distances that are becoming the standard for athletic competition the world over.

Bibliography

A junior high that's more than a school, American School and University 45:30, March, 1973.

American Association for Health, Physical Education and Recreation: Dressing rooms and related service facilities for physical education, athletics, and recreation, Washington, D.C., 1972, The Association.

Ashton, Dudley, and Irey, Charlotte, editors: Dance facilities, Washington, D.C., 1972, Council for Facilities, Equipment and Supplies, American Association for Health, Physical Education and Recreation.

Athletic Institute: Planning areas and facilities for health, physical education, and recreation by participants in National Facilities Conference, Chicago, 1974, The Institute.

Bronzan, Robert T.: New concepts in planning and funding athletic, physical education and recreation facilities, St. Paul, Minn., 1974, Phoenix Intermedia, Inc.

Browne, Robert Lee: Innovations in sports facilities, American School and University 44:24-30, Nov., 1971.

Bucher, Charles A.: Administration of health and physical education programs, including athletics, ed. 6, St. Louis, 1975, The C. V. Mosby Co.

College and university facilities guide, Chicago, 1968, The Athletic Institute and American Association for Health, Physical Education and Recreation.

Dexter, Genevie, and Early, Doyt: Facilities and space allocations for physical education outdoor teaching stations for elementary and intermediate public schools, Sacramento, Calif., 1967, California State Department of Education.

Dickey, Donald D.: Athletic lockers for schools and colleges: their design, selection, and purchase with functional tips and suggestions for the modern athletic locker room, Bloomington, Minn., 1967, Donald D. Dickey.

Educational Facilities Laboratories, Inc.: Conventional gymnasium vs. geodesic field house: a comparative study of high school physical education and assembly facilities, New York, 1961, EFL.

Educational Facilities Laboratories: Physical recreation facilities, New York, 1973, EFL.

Ezersky, Eugene M.: Mini-gyms and fitness corners, Journal of Health, Physical Education and Recreation 43:38-39, Jan., 1972.

Ezersky, Eugene, and Theibert, P. Richard: City schools without gyms, Journal of Health, Physical Education and Recreation 41:26-29, April, 1970.

Gabrielsen, M. Alexander, editor: Swimming pools: a guide to their planning, design and operation, Washington, D.C., 1974, Council for National Cooperation in Aquatics.

Let's look at new sports areas, American School and University 40:17, Aug., 1968.

Lightweight structures, Michigan City, Ind., 1972, Shaver & Co.

Lightweight structures for education, American School and University 45:27-30, July, 1973.

Moriarty, R. J.: PERT planning for physical education facilities, Canadian Association of Health, Physical Education and Recreation Journal 39:33-36, Aug., 1973.

Once in a lifetime sport facility, Scholastic Coach 42:48, Jan., 1973.

Planning facilities for athletics, physical education and recreation, 1974, The Athletic Institute and American Association for Health, Physical Education and Recreation.

P. Richard Theibert on facilities for lifetime sports: an interview, American School and University 44:14-18, Nov., 1971.

Ragsdale, Lee, and others: Dressing rooms and related service facilities for physical education, athletics and recreation, Washington, D.C., 1972, Council for Facilities, Equipment, and Supplies, American Association for Health, Physical Education and Recreation.

Smoll, Frank L.: Areas and facilities for physical education and recreation: an interpretive bibliography, Madison, Wisc., 1970, ERIC Clearinghouse on Educational Facilities, University of Wisconsin.

Theibert, P. Richard: A primer on synthetic surfaces, American School and University 43:44-45, Aug., 1971.

Appendix A

SUGGESTED LIST OF INITIAL EQUIPMENT AND SUPPLIES
FOR NEW HIGH SCHOOLS
(Health and Physical Education)

The following list was prepared by Mr. Bernard Kirschenbaum, Assistant Director of the Bureau for Health and Physical Education for the New York City Public Schools. It was developed for new coeducational high schools for New York City, built to accommodate approximately 4000 students.

Betadine skin cleanser, 4 oz.	cont.	12
Alcohol, isopropyl, 70% pt. in plastic cont.	pint	12
Applicators, wooden, 6 in. long (864 in box)	box	2
Gauze, bandage, 1 in., 10 yd. (12 in box)	box	4
Gauze, bandage, 2 in., 10 yd. (12 in box)	box	4
Bandage, 40 in., triangular bleached muslin	each	6
Utility blanket, 62 in. by 41 in., wool, 2½ lb.	each	4
Compress, adhesive elastic, ¾ in. by 2½ in.	each	100
Compress, 3 in. by 3 in., 100 in package	package	10
Cotton, sanitary absorbent, sterilized	box	6
Cotton, sanitary absorbent, unsterilized	roll	6
Tongue depressors, wooden, box of 500	cont.	4
First aid kit, 10-unit case	each	4
Forceps, splinters, plain, 3 in.	each	4
Forceps, thumb, plain, 5 in.	each	4
Gauze, absorbent, 25 yd., 4½ in. wide	box	4
Adhesive plaster, 5 yd., 1 in., box/12 rolls	box	10
Adhesive plaster, 5 yd., 2 in., box/12 rolls	box	10
Splint kit, complete w/case	case	2
Charts, eye test, mounted	each	4
Goggles, safety, plastic	pair	12
Lens, replacement, clear	pair	4
Coin sorter, manual	each	1
Bat rack	each	2
Bases, baseball	set	2
Home plate	each	2
Pitcher's box	each	2
Blocking dummies	each	6
Hand air dummies	each	6
Linesman's outfit, down marker	each	1
Football yard line markers	set	2

first aid

Goal flags	set	1
Stick, field hockey	each	20
Ball, aeracel field hockey	each	10
Goalie pads, field hockey	pair	2
Shin guards, field hockey	pair	20
Field marker, dry	each	1
Signal horn	each	1
Gas tank, signal horn	each	1
Corner flags	set	1
Tennis server	each	1
Tennis retriever	each	1
Vaulting pole, 12 ft.	each	2
Vaulting pole, 15 ft.	each	2
Vaulting pole, 16 ft.	each	2
4 base unit, pole vault pit	each	4
Front unit, pole vault pit	each	1
Top landing cushion, pole vault pit	each	1
All weather cover, pole vault pit	each	1
3 base unit, high jump pit	each	3
Top landing cushion, high jump pit	each	1
All weather cover, high jump pit	each	1
Standards, pole vault	pair	1
Standards, high jump	pair	1
Shot, outdoor (men)	each	2
Shot, indoor (men)	each	2
Take off board	each	2
Vaulting box, steel, outdoor	each	1
Shotput toe board	each	1
Steel measuring tape, 100 ft.	each	1
Stopwatch, 9-jewel	each	2
Starting block, adjustable	each	6
Starting block, mallet	each	2
Batons, silver finish	dozen	1
Batons, gold	dozen	1
Cross bar, aluminum, 16 ft.	set	1
Gun, starting, 22 caliber	each	2
Blanks, 22 caliber	box	10
Hurdles, adjustable	each	48
Tennis net, 42 ft.	each	4
Rack, vaulting pole	each	1
Emergency, "ready-splint"	case	1
Bullhorn, battery operated	each	1
Traffic cone, 18 in.	each	24
Tape measure, linen, 50 ft.	each	2
Timer, manual	each	2
Bolt clippers	each	2
Barbell set	set	10
Softball batting tee	each	4
Bowlite set	set	2
Paddles, paddle tennis	each	12
Badminton rackets, steel strung	each	30
Pump, table model	each	2

Physical fitness achievement board	each	2
Intramural records board	each	2
Splints, inflatable (complete in case)	kit	2
Stretcher, folding	each	2
Port-A-Score, indoor	each	1
Ready nets w/supports	each	2
Rebound nets, complete, 10 ft.	each	2
Training bag	each	1
Rack for storing barbells	each	4
Cage ball, 30 in. diam.	each	1
Table tennis table	each	2
Bench, under chinning bar	each	4
Floor tape laying machine	each	1
Low balance beam, 12 ft. by 4 in. by 12 in.	each	2
Low parallel bars	each	2
Illuminated eye chart, Model A	each	1
Lamp, spotlight w/12 in. flexible neck (medical office)	each	2
Audiometer, complete w/operating accessories	each	1
Scale, anthropometric, medical office	each	2
Standiometer, wood 37 in. to 71 in.	each	4
Stopwatch, 7-jewel, $^1/_5$ second, etc.	each	10
Physical fitness record, individual (100)	package	10
Physical fitness record, class (100)	package	5
Physical fitness record, cumulative (100)	package	10
Emergency room, boys and girls, pads (100)	package	20
Boys and girls transmissions envelopes (250)	cont.	2
Health record envelopes, boys (250)	cont.	10
Health record envelopes, girls (250)	cont.	10
Emergency home contact card, boys and girls (250)	package	10
Pressure-sensitive tape, green, no. 471, 1 in.	roll	6
Pressure-sensitive tape, red, no. 471, 1 in.	roll	6
Pressure-sensitive tape, green, no. 471, 1½ in.	roll	6
Pressure-sensitive tape, red, no. 471, 1½ in.	roll	6
Pressure-sensitive tape, yellow, no. 471, 1½ in.	roll	6
Pressure-sensitive tape, red, no. 471, 2 in.	roll	6
Pressure-sensitive tape, yellow, no. 471, 2 in.	roll	6
Pressure-sensitive tape, green, no. 471, 2 in.	roll	6
Scissors, 5½ in.	each	4
Bladder, striking bag	each	6
Striking bag	each	3
Striking bag, swivel	each	6
Golf balls, plastic	dozen	12
Golf balls, regulation	dozen	6
Ball, paddle tennis, 2½ in. sponge rubber	each	24
Rubber balls (handballs), box/12	box	6
Tennis ball, cont. of 3	cont.	40
Bases, indoor, 12 in. sq. vinyl plastic	set	4
Basketball, rubber, box/3	box	12
Bat, polyethylene, 29 in.	each	6
Bat, softball, lightweight	each	12
Softball bat, wooden 33 in. to 34 in.	each	12
Baton, aluminum, for track relays, package 12	package	4

Golf club, ladies, no. 2 wood	each	12
Golf club, ladies, no. 5 iron	each	12
Golf club, mens, no. 2 wood	each	12
Golf club, mens, no. 5 iron	each	12
Putter, men's and ladies	each	12
Indian clubs	pair	6
Putting disc	each	12
Football, rubber box/3	box	6
Glove, catcher's, softball	each	6
Glove, fielder's	each	20
Glove, fielder's, southpaw	each	6
Gloves, striking bag	pair	6
Mask, catcher's, softball	each	4
Net, badminton	each	8
Net, basketball, extra heavy nylon	pair	12
Net, tennis, 42 in. by 3 ft., rope cable, long (indoor and outdoor)	each	6
Net, volleyball (indoor use)	each	12
Bat tip protector rubber, box/12	box	2
Chest protector, softball	each	4
Tennis racket, mens, nylon	each	30
Tennis rackets, ladies, nylon	each	30
Rope, jump, 8 ft.	each	10
Rope, jump, 20 ft.	each	3
Shuttlecock, badminton, plastic, box/3	box	12
Soccerball, rubber, box/3	box	12
Softball, clincher type	each	12
Softball, polyethylene, 12 in. circ.	box/12	3
Softball, soft, box/6	box	6
Softball, girls, box/6	box	6
Ball, 6 in carton (table tennis)	cont.	24
Net and attachments, table tennis	each	6
Paddle (rubber covered wooden), table tennis	each	24
Tumbling belt	each	4
Volleyball, rubber, box/3	box	12
Ball carrier, nylon (to carry basketballs, etc.)	each	4
Ball carrier, nylon (to carry small balls)	each	4
Ball carrier (on wheels, for indoor use)	each	4
Activity calendar, 24 in. by 36 in., weekly	each	2
Dance drum and beater	each	2
Dance drum beater, lamb's wool head	each	2
Horn referee, nickel-plated	each	4
Chart, inventory control system	set	2
Magnesium carbonate, 2 oz. cont., package/8	package	50
Rubber mats, ¼ in. thick, 5 ft. by 6 ft. used for barbells	each	6
Pinnies, blue	each	20
Pinnies, green	each	20
Pinnies, red	each	20
Pinnies, white	each	20
Pinnies, yellow	each	20
Cleaner for posters and charts, 4 oz. plastic bottle	bottle	2
Pencils for marking Eraso posters, assorted (12)	box	2

Eraso standing poster, 14 in. by 22 in. (basketball)	each	2
Eraso standing poster, 14 in. by 22 in. (softball)	each	2
Eraso posters, announcements	each	2
Stencil set, 5 in., letters and numbers	each	2
Peg board climber, 32 in. by 32 in.		2
Peg board climber, 20 in. by 60 in.		2
Horizontal bar, adjustable height, wall-mounted, semiguyed		2
Horizontal bar, fully guyed		1
Chinning bar, adjustable height		2
Climbing ropes, sets of 4	sets	2
Still rings, self-hoist type	pairs	2
Traveling rings, self-hoist type, set of 4	set	1
Horizontal bar spotting belt suspension		1
Permanent spotting belt suspension		1
Twisting belt, sizes 24 in. to 32 in., 30 in. and over		2
Heavy training bag		1
Striking bag drum		1
Multipurpose standards, portable		8
Trampoline, flash fold		1
Parallel bars, regulation		2
Uneven parallel bars		2
Side horse		2
Vaulting horse		2
Transporter, parallels and horse		2
Balance beam, regulation with pad		1
Transporter, balance beam	pair	1
Reuther board, padded, with spacer		2
Chalk stand		2
Combination wrestling–free exercise mat, 42 in. by 42 in.		1
Transporter, wrestling–free exercise mat	pair	1
Cut-out mats, parallels, unevens, horse, 6 ft. by 12 ft.		8
Cut-out mat, balance beam		1
Mat, 5 ft. by 8 ft. by 2 in.		36
Mat, folding, 5 ft. by 10 ft. by 2 in.		12
Mat, landing, 6 ft. by 12 ft. by 4 in.		2
Mat, broad jump, 3 ft. by 12 ft., with marking		2
Hurdles, adjustable height		12
Cross bars		6
Chalkboard, portable		2
Score flashers, portable		1
Scoreboard, electric		1

Storage facilities for mats (either hooks, portable trucks, Velcro strips, etc.)

Appendix B

SPACE REQUIREMENTS FOR PHYSICAL EDUCATION AND ATHLETIC COMPLEX*

The following checklists are intended for use in the early stages of planning for any new facility. By making realistic projections as to the space requirements necessary to accommodate the multitude of activities to be offered at the facility, professional physical educators can better communicate their facility needs to the architect. These checklists should be used before any drawings are made.

*Courtesy Richard Hawley Cutting & Associates, Inc.

Re: _____   Date _____
                          (SCHOOL)   Information supplied by:
_____
                          (LOCATION)   _____

ATHLETIC COMPLEX
Space requirements

OFFICES

	Facility no.	Suggested total sq. ft.
Number required		
Dean		
Chairman @ 150 sq. ft. each (1 occupant)		
Faculty @ 100 sq. ft. each (1 occupant)		
Faculty @ 160 sq. ft. each (swimming instruction)		
Faculty @ 200 sq. ft. each (4 graduate assistants in each)		
Faculty @ 100 sq. ft. each (2 graduate assistants in each)		
Receptionist and typist		
Typist and intramural scheduling office		
Building scheduling office		
Swimming general control office		

CLASSROOMS

	Facility no.	Suggested total sq. ft.
Number required		
Seminar @ 400 sq. ft. each (20 students @ 20 sq. ft. each)		
Lecture (30 students @ 14 sq. ft. each)		
Lecture @ 680 sq. ft. each (40 students @ 17 sq. ft. each)		

CLASSROOMS	Facility no.	Suggested total sq. ft.
Number required		
Lecture @ 600 sq. ft. (50 students @ 12 sq. ft. each) ...		
Lecture @ 720 sq. ft. (60 students @ 12 sq. ft. each) ...		
Lecture @ 1200 sq. ft. each (100 students @ 12 sq. ft. each)		

LABORATORY CLASSROOMS

Gymnasium type A, 110 ft. by 40 ft. or 2 50 ft. by 94 ft. courts ....
Gymnasium type B, 70 ft. by 96 ft. or 2 50 ft. by 75 ft. courts
Dance classroom type A, 56 ft. by 56 ft. ....
Dance classroom type B, 34 ft. by 42 ft. ....
Swimming pool type A (including deck area), pool 42 ft. by 75 ft. ....
Swimming pool type B (including deck area), pool 75 by 25 meters ....
Swimming pool type C (including deck area), pool 75 by 50 meters ....
Exercise therapy, 50 ft. by 50 ft. (corrective adaptive) ..
Gymnastics gymnasium, 60 ft. by 90 ft. ....
Treatment and training room ....
Progressive resistance exercise, 40 ft. by 60 ft. ....
Handball courts, 23 ft. by 46 ft. (6 @ 1058 sq. ft. each) ..
Squash courts, 18 ft. and 6 in. by 32 ft. and 0 in. singles . 25 ft. and 0 in. by 45 ft. and 0 in. doubles ....
Wrestling, 40 ft. by 80 ft. ....

DRESSING ROOMS **Number of students at peak hour**

Women's physical education and intramural
Locker and dressing area ....
Shower and toweling area ....
Lavatory and toilet area ....
Hair drying and make-up area ....
Towel and uniform issue room ....
Women's faculty locker, dressing, and shower area ...
Women's swimming instructor shower and locker room
Men's physical education and intramural
Locker and dressing area ....
Shower ....
Toweling area ....
Lavatory and toilet area ....
Towel and uniform issue room ....
Men's faculty locker, dressing, shower, and toweling area
Men's swimming instructor shower and locker room ..

Intercollegiate athletics—locker requirements **Size and number of teams**

Football-baseball ....
Soccer-lacrosse ....
Basketball ....
Swimming ....
Track ....

Intercollegiate athletics—locker requirements

Size and number
of teams

Wrestling ....
Tennis ....
Golf ....
Coaches' locker, dressing, and shower area ....

OTHER ROOMS

First aid room ....
Swimming pool equipment storage ....
Dance property storage ....
Costume construction and storage ....
Field and equipment storage ....
Canoe storage ....
Ski storage ....
Women's physical education department storage room A
Women's physical education department storage room B
Recreation department storage ....
Intramural equipment storage room ....
Gymnasium equipment storage ....
Gymnasium supervision and equipment issue room ...
Gallery swimming pool A (40 seats @ 7 sq. ft. each) ...
Gallery swimming pool B (1000 seats @ 5 sq. ft. each) .
Gallery gymnasium A (200 seats @ 6 sq. ft. each) ......
Gallery gymnasium B (200 seats @ 6 sq. ft. each) ......
Gallery dance classroom A (100 seats @ 9 sq. ft. each) .
Athletic uniforms and equipment issue room ....
Athletic equipment storage ....
Athletic off-season equipment storage ....
Athletic equipment repair room ....
Student group study room ....
Student quiet study room ....
Faculty conference room ....
Staff duplicating machine and work room ....
Photo darkroom (physical therapy) ....
Physical therapy storage room ....
Audiovisual equipment storage room ....
Audio and television central control room ....
Press boxes ....
Laundry ....
Towel and uniform storage room ....
Scuba equipment ....

FOOTBALL

Quantity	Equipment	Unit	Total space
	Game jerseys	30 @ 24 in. H by 13 in. W by 17 in. D	
	Practice jerseys	30 @ 24 in. H by 13 in. W by 17 in. D	
	Game pants	15 @ 18 in. H by 12 in. W by 17 in. D	
	Practice pants	15 @ 18 in. H by 12 in. W by 17 in. D	
	Thigh pads	20 pair @ 28 in. H by 15 in. W by 12 in. D	
	Hip pads (regular)	6 pair @ 18 in. H by 14 in. W by 16 in. D	
	Hip pads (girdle)		
	Helmets	1 @ 11 in. H by 10 in. W by 13 in. D	
	Regular shoulder pads	8 @ 40 in. H by 30 in. W by 18 in. D (on shoulder)	
	Big boy shoulder pads	4 @ 40 in. H by 30 in. W by 18 in. D (pad rack)	
	Warm-up jackets	6 @ 18 in. H by 14 in. W by 16 in. D	
	Shoes (new)	8 pair @ 17 in. H by 14 in. W by 13 in. D	
	Shoes (used)		
	Knee pads	8 pair @ 11 in. H by 12 in. W by 11 in. D	
	Game stockings	20 pair @ 20 in. H by 6 in. W by 20 in. D	
	Rib pads	8 pair @ 16 in. H by 13 in. W by 16 in. D	
	Rain capes (wool)		
	Rain capes (rubber)		
	Belts		
	Kicking tees and toes		
	Thermal undershirts		
	Frosh game pants		
	Frosh game jerseys		
	Goal line flags		
	Footballs		
	Traveling bags		
	Scrimmage vests		

LACROSSE

Quantity	Equipment	Unit	Total space
	Helmet	1 @ 11 in. H by 10 in. W by 13 in. D	
	Shoes	8 pair @ 17 in. H by 14 in. W by 13 in. D	
	Shoulder pads	6 pair @ 12 in. H by 16 in. W by 28 in. D	
	Arm pads		
	Gloves	6 pair @ 12 in. H by 14 in. W by 16 in. D	
	Sticks (bin)	100 @ 42 in. H by 60 in. W by 36 in. D	
	Shorts	20 pair @ 20 in. H by 12 in. W by 15 in. D	
	Goalie cups	6 @ 18 in. H by 8 in. W by 16 in. D	
	Cup supporters		
	Chest protectors		
	Sweat pants		
	Game jackets		
	Game jerseys		
	Practice jerseys		

BASEBALL

Quantity	Equipment	Unit	Total space
	Shirts	15 @ 19 in. H by 14 in. W by 17 in. D	
	Pants	15 pair @ 18 in. H by 12 in. W by 17 in. D	
	Undershirts	12 @ 12 in. H by 12 in. W by 14 in. D	
	Stockings	20 pair @ 20 in. H by 6 in. W by 20 in. D	
	Sanitary socks	20 pair @ 10 in. H by 6 in. W by 20 in. D	
	Shoes	8 pair @ 17 in. H by 14 in. W by 13 in. D	
	Neck warmers	20 @ 20 in. H by 10 in. W by 19 in. D	
	Game jackets	6 @ 18 in. H by 14 in. W by 16 in. D	
	Caps	20 @ 20 in. H by 9 in. W by 12 in. D	
	Belts		
	Catcher's shin guard		
	Catcher's chest protector		
	Bats		
	Ball bags		
	Bat bags		
	Catcher's mitts		
	Rubber shirts		
	Batting helmets		
	Fungo bats		
	Baseballs		
	Traveling bags		

SOCCER

Quantity	Equipment	Unit	Total space
	Jerseys	30 @ 24 in. H by 13 in. W by 17 in. D	
	Shorts	20 pair @ 20 in. H by 12 in. W by 15 in. D	
	Shin guards	10 pair @ 12 in. H by 11 in. W by 11 in. D	
	Stockings	20 pair @ 20 in. H by 6 in. W by 20 in. D	
	Shoes	8 pair @ 17 in. H by 14 in. W by 13 in. D	
	Warm-up jackets	6 @ 18 in. H by 14 in. W by 16 in. D	
	Hoods	6 @ 19 in. H by 13 in. W by 15 in. D	
	Balls (rack)	6 @ 22 in. H by 21 in. W by 13 in. D	
	Shin guards		
	Nets (goal)		
	Traveling bags		

BASKETBALL

Quantity	Equipment	Unit	Total space
	Practice shorts	20 pair @ 20 in. H by 12 in. W by 15 in. D	
	Game shorts	20 pair @ 20 in. H by 12 in. W by 15 in. D	
	Game jerseys	20 @ 20 in. H by 14 in. W by 17 in. D	
	Practice jerseys	20 @ 20 in. H by 14 in. W by 17 in. D	
	Warm-up pants	6 @ 15 in. H by 12 in. W by 18 in. D	
	Shoes	8 pair @ 17 in. H by 14 in. W by 19 in. D	
	Warm-up jackets	6 @ 18 in. H by 14 in. W by 16 in. D	
	Balls (rack)	6 @ 32 in. H by 21 in. W by 13 in. D	
	Traveling bags		

TENNIS

Quantity	Equipment	Unit	Total space
	Shirts (game and practice)		
	Shorts		
	Shoes		
	Warmer jackets		
	Warmer pants		
	Balls		
	Nets		

WRESTLING

Quantity	Equipment	Unit	Total space
	Practice tights	15 @ 20 in. H by 10 in. W by 14 in. D	
	Overtights	20 @ 18 in. H by 9 in. W by 14 in. D	
	Meet and practice shoes	8 pair @ 17 in. H by 14 in. W by 13 in. D	
	Knee pads	8 pair @ 11 in. H by 12 in. W by 11 in. D	
	Head gear	10 @ 18 in. H by 6 in. W by 14 in. D	
	Meet tights	15 @ 20 in. H by 10 in. W by 14 in. D	
	Meet overtights	20 @ 18 in. H by 9 in. W by 14 in. D	
	Meet jackets	6 @ 18 in. H by 14 in. W by 16 in. D	
	Rubber shirts		
	Traveling bags		
	Warm-up jackets		

TRACK

Quantity	Equipment	Unit	Total space
	Meet jerseys	20 @ 18 in. H by 15 in. W by 15 in. D	
	Practice jerseys		
	Meet shorts	20 pair @ 20 in. H by 12 in. W by 15 in. D	
	Practice shorts		
	Shoes	8 pair @ 17 in. H by 14 in. W by 13 in. D	
	Sweat shirts (meet and practice)	6 @ 14 in. H by 12 in. W by 16 in. D	
	Sweat pants (meet and practice)	6 @ 14 in. H by 12 in. W by 16 in. D	
	Hoods	6 @ 19 in. H by 13 in. W by 15 in. D	
	Traveling bags		
	Discus		
	Javelins		
	Shotputs		

GOLF

Quantity	Equipment	Unit	Total space
	Shirts		
	Warmer jackets		
	Balls		

GENERAL EQUIPMENT

Quantity	Equipment	Unit	Total space
	Thermal undershirts	12 @ 12 in. H by 12 in. W by 14 in. D	
	Inner gear	56 rolls @ 16 in. H by 24 in. W by 24 in. D	
	Towels	50 @ 16 in. H by 21 in. W by 19 in. D	
	Shorts (practice)	20 pair @ 20 in. H by 12 in. W by 15 in. D	
	Traveling bags	5 @ 18 in. H by 20 in. W by 22 in. D	
	Rain caps	5 @ 20 in. H by 17 in. W by 22 in. D	
	Sweat shirts	6 @ 14 in. H by 12 in. W by 16 in. D	
	Sweat pants	6 @ 14 in. H by 12 in. W by 16 in. D	
	Hoods	6 @ 19 in. H by 13 in. W by 15 in. D	

INTRAMURALS AND PHYSICAL EDUCATION

Quantity	Equipment	Unit	Total space
	Softball bats		
	Softball marks		
	Softballs		
	Handball gloves		
	Handballs		
	Volleyballs		
	Soccer balls		
	Tennis rackets		
	Tennis balls		
	Softball bases		
	Basketball nets		
	Badminton rackets		
	Badminton birds		
	Sweat shirts		
	Sweat pants		
	Golf clubs		
	Footballs		
	Golf balls		

Appendix C

ROOM BY ROOM DETAILED PROGRAMMING DOCUMENT*

Room identifier													Date										Prof		Plumbing														
						Room																				Number		Yes/No (1 or 0)												
Building number				Floor		Number						Surface	Day		Month		Year		Number				Floor	Ceiling	Lavatory	Sink	Shower	Urinal	Commode	Hot water	Cold water	Chilled water	Distilled water	Floor drain	Acid drain	Sprinkler	Air	Gas
1	2	3	4	5	6	7	8	9	10	11	12	13	14	15	16	17	18	19	20	21	22	23	24	25	26	27	28	29	30	31	32	33	34	35	36	37	38	39
1	2	3	4	5	6	7	8	9	10	11	12	13	14	15	16	17	18	19	20	21	22	23	24	25	26	27	28	29	30	31	32	33	34	35	36	37	38	39

*From Caudill Rowlett Scott, 1111 West Loop South, Houston, Texas 77027. To ensure completeness and accuracy of detail in the building process, this checklist should be completed for every room/space in the facility under consideration.

					Electrical Yes/No (1 or 0)													HVAC (1 or 0)						Y/N																C C
Vacuum	Oxygen	Nitrous oxide	Fire equipment	Other	Electrical outlet	Special outlet	Emergency outlet	D-C outlet	Incandescent light	Fluorescent light	Rheostat switch	A–V outlet	Telephone outlet	Intercom	CCTV	Fire box	Other	Radiator	Thermostat	Exhaust	Diffuser	Other	AC code	Chalkboard	Window	Type	Space													
40	41	42	43	44	45	46	47	48	49	50	51	52	53	54	55	56	57	58	59	60	61	62	63	64	65	66	67	68	69	70	71	72	73	74	75	76	77	78	79	80
40	41	42	43	44	45	46	47	48	49	50	51	52	53	54	55	56	57	58	59	60	61	62	63	64	65	66	67	68	69	70	71	72	73	74	75	76	77	78	79	80

Appendix D

EQUIPPING THE GYMNASTICS AREA*

The gymnastics area is highly specialized, and, depending on program emphasis, it can be as basic or sophisticated as necessary. This appendix lists basic competitive, instructional, support, and safety apparatus. Following the basic list is a selection of equipment common to and necessary for the development of a sound gymnastics program. Information about equipment and gymnastics activities is also included.

1. *Parallel bars.* They must be easily adjustable and equipped with a floating counterbalance mechanism in each upright for safety and convenience in making both height and width adjustments. The bars should be multilaminated without reinforcement rods inside.

   a. *Support apparatus—low parallel bars.* This piece of apparatus is ideal for safely learning the inverted balance positions common to parallel bar movements. The handstand, shoulderstand, etc., can be spotted conveniently by an assistant standing on the floor. Also, the performer can more readily gain confidence for these moves at the low height that these bars provide.

   b. *Training equipment.* For the more advanced moves it should be possible to locate the parallel bars underneath an overhead spotting device.

   c. *Safety provisions.* Mats should be placed under and completely around the parallel bars. A platform mat measuring 12 feet by 16 feet is recommended.

   d. *Teaching considerations.* It is important that the parallel bars have a full range of adjustment to account for the smallest to the largest student in the program. If the teacher training program is to involve the use of the facility by very young children, then a supplemental set of parallel bars designed specifically for them should be considered.

      Both ends of the bars may be used for the mass teaching of many of the skills, but for most effective instruction more than one unit should be available. Conversion kits for the women's uneven bars may provide an answer for this need.

---

*Reprinted with permission of the Nissen Corporation, Cedar Rapids, Iowa.

2. *Uneven bars.* Like the men's parallel bars, these bars should be easily adjustable to a wide range of width (432 to 813 mm.) and height adjustments on both the low (1450 to 1900 mm.) and the high (2000 to 2450 mm.) bars. This will allow for official meet specifications and will also provide a full range for younger students. It is even more important that the uneven bars be of fused laminated construction because the women's event places tremendous stress on the bars.

   a. *Support apparatus.* Many of the basic movements in this event may be practiced on a single bar. An easily adjustable men's horizontal bar set at the height of the low bar will provide an additional instructional station.

   b. *Training equipment.* A fully padded spotting platform will be an asset for the instructor as an aid in assisting a student on the top bar.

   c. *Safety provisions.* Movements on the uneven bars occur at right angles to the longitudinal axis of the apparatus. Mats should be placed under the apparatus and in line with this movement. Three 6 foot by 12 foot 1¼ inch roll-fold mats to provide for safe dismounts and two 6 foot by 12 inch by 4 inch landing mats placed in the dismount areas should be used.

   d. *Teaching considerations.* For many of the beginning moves two performers may use the apparatus at the same time. However, for more efficient mass instruction, additional stations should be provided. With a conversion kit for the men's bars, a second station may be found. Also, providing the equipment is available, one bar may be removed from the men's bars, and the horizontal bar may be lowered to provide a station for single-bar work.

3. *Balance beam.* The beam should meet all International Federation of Gymnastics specifications and should be fully adjustable from 33½ to 52½ inches. This adjustment should be such that it may be easily accomplished by one girl. The construction of the wood beam should be of opposing laminations to neutralize the effect of expansion and contraction. A roughened, non-skid, lacquer surface should be provided for safe footing.

   a. *Support apparatus.* A lower training beam with the same official surface should be used as a transitional beam as the girls gain confidence.

   b. *Training equipment.* A pair of training pads, fitted about the beam, should be used as an aid in learning such skills as the backward roll, handstands, and in converting the beam to a vaulting station.

   c. *Safety provisions.* Protective mats must be placed on each side of the beam (two 6 feet by 16 feet by 1¼ inches), as well as on each end where dismounts occur (two 6 feet by 12 feet by 1¼ inches). For the more advanced dismounts a 6 foot by 12 foot by 4 inch landing mat should be provided.

   d. *Teaching considerations.* For mass teaching of the basic balance skills and traveling movements, lines painted on the floor may be used. These skills may then be transferred to the training beam and finally to the official beam.

4. *Side horse, vaulting horse, and long horse.* This piece of apparatus must meet exacting Olympic specifications. It must easily adjust from 40 to 60 inches in height and quickly convert from side horse (with pommels) to vaulting horse (without pommels) and be able to be raised to become a long horse. The base support must be solid to meet the demands of each event.

   a. *Support apparatus.* For teaching basic side horse skills, two additional pieces of apparatus are useful. A training horse with the same pommel and top specifications will provide additional practice time for the basic side horse moves. A short horse (a buck with pommels) is of value as an intermediate piece for teaching many side horse movements. With the pommels off, this piece of equipment becomes an asset for the vaulting program.

   As an aid to teaching the vaulting events, the vaulting box with adjustable, removable tiers is of great value.

   b. *Training equipment.* For providing positive spotting and instilling confidence, the overhead traveling suspension is an important device for mastering the more advanced vaulting skills.

   c. *Safety provisions.* The side horse event requires a level, protective mat area surrounding the apparatus. A 12 foot by 12 foot by 3 inch platform mat meets this requirement.

   For the women's vaulting event a 6 foot by 18 foot by 1¼ inch roll-fold base mat and a 6 foot by 12 foot by 4 inch landing mat are needed.

   The men's long horse vaulting event requires the wider 8 foot by 18 foot by 1¼ inch roll-fold base mat, together with an 8 foot by 18 foot by 4 inch landing mat.

   d. *Teaching considerations.* Although one piece of apparatus can be adapted to each of the three events, three horses must be available for an efficient instructional program. Three horses will allow simultaneous individual work at each station, and by quickly converting all to a single purpose, effective mass teaching techniques can be employed.

5. *Rings.* For official competition and for consistent action, the rings must be suspended exactly 18 feet from the floor. The best answer to this is to be had in the portable ring frame. This frame is guyed to the floor with four cables anchored in floor plates.

   a. *Support apparatus.* The official competitive rings are set approximately 8 feet off the floor with only minor height adjustments possible. For the instructional program there are many advantages to be gained by installing the fully adjustable self-hoist rings.

b. *Safety provisions.* Centered under the rings should be an 8 foot by 18 foot by 1¼ inch roll-fold mat, together with an 8 foot by 12 foot by 4 inch landing mat.

6. *Horizontal bar.* International Federation of Gymnastics specifications call for the bar to be approximately 8 feet in length and 1.105 inches in diameter. During competitive routines this bar must withstand tremendous strains. To continue to give top performance and to meet complete safety standards, it should be heat treated with a 100% certified minimal tensile strength of 200,000 psi. Guy cables and floor attachments should also be able to withstand any performing pressures.

a. *Support apparatus.* For effective teaching, there should be available an additional bar that can be quickly adjusted to the low bar position.

b. *Training equipment.* Two types of suspended training belts are an aid to instruction on the horizontal bar. One type attaches directly to the ends of the bar with 360-degree ball bearing fittings. The other ends of the ropes are attached to the performer's waist. This prevents the performer from falling to the floor should his grip fail. The second type of suspension that should be available is an overhead suspension that would be used for assisting dismounts. This would be attached to the ceiling over and slightly ahead of the bar. A padded spotter's platform that allows the instructor to be in a more efficient position for spotting the performer above the bar is another aid to instruction.

c. *Safety provisions.* The horizontal bar requires a rather long floor area to be protectively covered. Two 18 foot by 8 foot by 1¼ inch roll-fold base mats should be centered under the bar. In the area of the dismount there should be an 8 foot by 12 foot by 4 inch landing mat.

d. *Teaching considerations.* All advanced horizontal bar moves are accomplished with the bar set 8 feet above the floor. Beginning moves and many of the "in-bar" moves are first learned with the bar set in the low-bar position (approximately 5 feet above the floor). Horizontal bar stations at each height should be available for efficient instruction. Official bars are 8 feet wide. No bar should be less than this because this length makes it possible for beginning skills to be taught two at a time at all horizontal bar stations for mass teaching.

7. *Free exercise.* This event requires a clear 42 foot by 42 foot mat area. The mat surface should be continuous, with no cracks, and should be of a consistency that a performer has a cushioned landing, yet is not so resilient as to prevent adequate lift.

a. *Support apparatus.* Additional mats to provide a practice tumbling run (6 feet by 60 feet) should be available in addition to the 42 foot by 42 foot area.

b. *Training equipment.* For the more advanced tumbling moves, a traveling suspension is of value. A 6 foot by 12 foot by 12 inch landing pad is also needed to learn these moves.

Multiuse equipment

The following equipment is needed as indicated for several or all gymnastics events.

1. *Trampolines.* Perhaps the greatest contribution to any gymnastics program is the trampoline. This popular piece of apparatus allows the beginner to meet success the first day, and for this reason it attracts and holds students to the sport. Its challenge is endless and provides the possibility for the multiple twisting, multiple somersaulting moves that are responsible for the rapid rise in the degree of difficulty of the horizontal bar dismounts, free exercise moves, and complex long horse vaults. The trampoline is indispensible for the development of any gymnastic program whether it be the very beginning or most advanced.

2. *Strength-building equipment.* One of the greatest limiting factors to success in gymnastics is lack of strength for the attempted move. There are several pieces of equipment that should be included in the program to provide for the development of this necessary ingredient for success.

    a. *Climbing ropes.* Climbing skills should be taught and the ropes made available so that climbing is a part of every gymnastic workout.

    b. *Wall-attached chinning bars.* Exercises for upper arm development can be accomplished on the regular horizontal bars, but a wall-mounted chinning bar can readily be available for this essential developmental work.

    c. *Wall-mounted parallel bars.* This piece of apparatus can be used to great advantage for development of the upper arms, shoulders, and abdominal strength. All are essential to gymnastic success.

3. *Reuther boards.* This is a necessary piece of apparatus for several events. It is a take-off board for the vaulting events (for the men's vaulting a Reuther board spacer unit is also needed) and may be used to assist in mounting the other apparatus. Several should be on hand for efficient use.

4. *Mini-tramps.* These are small portable trampolines used to spring performers for vaults, somersaults, etc. They are of value for the beginning vaulting program and the tumbling free exercise events as well. It is an exciting piece of apparatus that students enjoy because it provides a means of meeting success before all aspects of a complex skill are mastered.

5. *Safety belts.* These belts are used about the waist while attempting somersaulting skills. With short ropes, two spotters hold the performer while he attempts a new move. These ropes may also be used with the overhead suspensions, in which one spotter can completely control the performer. Two types of these belts should be available: the standard, lightweight, strong, nylon, fully adjustable belt for simple, nontwisting moves and the two-part twisting belt in which the performer is free to

rotate on two different planes at the same time. An adequate number of both of these belts should be available.

6. *Miscellaneous supplies.* Several minor items make a gymnastic program complete.

   a. *Chalk trays.* Several of these items should be placed about the workout area so that a gymnast can conveniently chalk his hands before mounting an apparatus. Chalk on the hands is a must for safety, and well-designed trays conveniently located will be an asset to the program.

   b. *Mat trucks.* In most instances, gymnasiums are multiuse facilities, and the floor must be cleared. Flat mat trucks designed to carry the folded mats to the storage area make this task much easier.

   c. *Port-A-Scores.* For gymnastic meets, a fast, convenient method of flashing the competitor's score is needed. By far, the best answer to this need is the blinker type of score flasher. These units may also be used in the instructional program, as well as in other sports activities.

   d. *Instructional aids.* Visual presentation of instructional material is of great value to the advancement of gymnastics. Wall charts, films, and books should be readily available to the prospective learner.

Basic equipment

Following is a list of basic equipment necessary for the gymnastics area:

Quantity	Equipment
2	Horizontal bars
1	Parallel bar
1	Low parallel bar
1	Uneven bar
1	Beam
1	Training beam
1 set	Balance beam training pads
3	Horses
1	Buck and short horse
1	Ring frame
1	Ring
2	Trampolines
2	Climbing ropes
1	Chinning bar
1	Wall parallel bar
2	Reuther boards
1	Reuther board training pad
1	Reuther board with carpeting
3	Mini-tramps
2	Permanent suspensions
1	Traveling suspension
1	Horizontal bar suspension
4	Spotting belts
1	Small twisting belt

Appendixes

Quantity	Equipment
1	Large twisting belt
3	Chalk stands
1	Vaulting box
3	Port-A-Scores
	Mats
5	6 feet by 12 feet roll-fold mats
2	6 feet by 16 feet roll-fold mats
1	6 feet by 18 feet roll-fold mat
4	8 feet by 18 feet roll-fold mats
1	Platform mat
4	Landing mats (6 feet by 12 feet by 4 inches)
3	Landing mats (8 feet by 12 feet by 4 inches)
1	Landing mat (6 feet by 12 feet by 12 inches)
1	Free exercise mat (42 feet by 42 feet)
	(*Note:* If men's and women's programs are held in separate facilities, two free exercise mats will be required.)

Appendix E

GOOFS IN ATHLETIC FACILITY CONSTRUCTION
(A lighthearted warning to our colleagues)

Material included in this appendix is excerpted from a talk frequently given to graduate classes in physical education by one of us (P.R.T.). The intended humor should not mask some very important considerations that are frequently overlooked in the planning and construction process.

. . . . The biggest goof you can make is to permit your leader to force you to accept the campus architect or a name architect. He didn't become world famous building physical education buildings.

. . . . If you must accept some trustee's brother or a politician's secretary, insist on hiring an outside consultant.

The reasons are simple—the following headline came from a big-city paper—"East addition old before it's finished." And from the same article, "524 letters from the contractor complaining about job specifications are on file in the Department of Public Works." If it is your building, familiarize yourself with all specifications before you start.

. . . . In your field everyone is a self-appointed expert—there are no real experts—some are a little better versed than others. No one has all the answers.

. . . . You can use the press, but again remember the "sportswriter" does not see the entire physical education picture, the campus master plan and philosophy, and/or the costs from the institution's perspective. He may be a superb critic or, conversely, be responsive only to the professional sports community.

. . . . Be careful of sightlines that prevent you from seeing the action. An example is the inability of spectators to see the near lane in a pool or part of the water surface because of window glare. No windows in a pool is preferable.

. . . . Recently completed pools have been made so narrow that records don't count or 8 inches too long, so that every race is a "bastard length." Check carefully—these are inexcusable errors.

. . . . When you count seats, don't count for today, count for ten years ahead. Build so extra seats can be added or subtracted. If possible, leave room on the ends for human safety. Seats are the first item that authorities cut back; they cannot obtain government funds for seats. Ask yourself if the cost of the seats merits the number of times bodies will be sitting in them.

. . . . Large garage doors should open into the major areas for trucks and busses. A visiting team can then unload near the proper area. This was carefully done in one new building, and when the trucks were unloaded, the players had to carry the equipment up three flights of stairs. Great exercise—with cleats; catastrophic and pretty treacherous even without cleats.

. . . . If you wish a psychological advantage over your opponent, put the broad jump pit along the wall. It's demoralizing when they scrape a boy off the wall.

. . . . Don't put pipes in a wall if it can be avoided. Picture a beautiful tile shower room with a broken shower pipe. What a mess! Maintenance will be a little high. Don't be too plush. The ratio of time between the locker room and recreational areas should favor the recreational area.

. . . . Check the lobby size. How many hours will you use it? Put this space into recreational use. People can purchase tickets standing under a roof. Princeton University can use their lobby for banquets, an excellent idea.

. . . . Check carefully all foot traffic paths—students, faculty, and spectator.

. . . . Take colored pencils and trace the path each person travels on the blueprints. If you find the paths cross continually or, as they did in one case, everyone walks through the muddiest areas, you will have a filthy building and need traffic cops. Request the architect to start over. Then, of course, there are the beautiful fields, but you stand in 6 inches of mud by the bench, probably the most common error. Buy some strips of synthetic materials.

. . . . Don't forget the world-famous example of the masterful piece of architecture and no water fountains. This may be good for concessionaires on game days, but it's a long, dry week. Tough on kids who can't drink beer. Not recommended for high schools and younger age groups.

. . . . Don't forget to slope the floors of shower rooms toward the drain, not away from it, as was done at a major university recently.

. . . . Why does a basketball court have to be smooth? The circumference of the ball is so large that the bounce is unaffected by a grained or pebbled surface. Now you can also use the area to perfection for other endeavors. We're faced with an old tradition—some pretty fair basketball players have come out of the asphalt leagues in New York and Los Angeles.

. . . . Insist on janitor closets on every level; it's tough carrying machinery and equipment up and down stairs. If you can afford several million for a building, you can afford an elevator.

. . . . Be sure you build doors into every room. It's very embarrassing to end up with a doorless room. Rumor was this recently happened in one of the world's most famous auditoriums, a dressing room without a door.

. . . . In a parking study take into account existing lots within walking distance. Are they used on Saturday night? Check—don't pay for extra lots. Apply this same thought to toilets; every piece of porcelain is $500 to $1500. Then, of course, there's the penthouse wrestling room. Matches were held four floors below. Moving mats was a weighty problem. Too many mistakes are made in the relationship of wrestling practice and meet areas.

. . . . Use ramps whenever you can; steps are a goof. You can move things on ramps. Ramps also move handicapped students more directly into the mainstream.

. . . . Don't build the top row of seats in an arena so close to the ceiling that when spectators jump up in excitement at the finish of a race, 500 heads literally hit the ceiling, which actually happened in one case.

. . . . Don't forget that an auditorium or arena is filled with thousands of people over a period of about 45 minutes before the event begins, but everyone wants to exit at the same time when the event is over. A world-famous indoor arena built a beautiful and aesthetic looking system of escalators to its various seating levels, adjacent to floor-to-ceiling plate glass exterior windows. This was practical and efficient when spectators entered, but hazardous on leaving. Guards and safeguards now have to be employed at the conclusion of almost every full-house attraction.

. . . . Don't overbuild on toilets. Some institutions have almost as many toilets as people.

. . . . Don't build single-purpose buildings and place multipurpose names on them. Some spectator seats are not used more than ten times a year. When seats are built, make sure there are enough bottoms around to fill these seats often enough to make it economically sound.

. . . . Don't forget to invite the students to participate in the planning of the facility. *All* students. When you're done with the facility and off to a new professional position, they'll inherit it—obsolescence and all—and obsolescence is usually only ten years away.

. . . . Don't forget to consult the many professional agencies that can contribute to your efforts. The initial list of initials is usually enough to scare you off, but persist. Among others, there are the NCAA, NAIA, AAU, NACDA, NEA, AAHPER, and HEW, plus all the individual sports organizations.

Appendix F

RECOMMENDED EQUIPMENT FOR ADAPTED PHYSICAL EDUCATION*

REMEDIAL EXERCISE EQUIPMENT

Stationary equipment
Physical training machine
Stall bars, 6-foot unit
Stall bar bench
Abdominal incline board (for stall bars)
Triplex pulley weights
Wrist roll machine
Wrist pronator-supinator
Shoulder wheel
Chinning bar
Parallel bars, wall-mounted
Pegboard
Movable equipment
Bicycle exerciser
Rowing machine
Ankle exerciser
Shoulder abduction ladder
Heel stretcher
Foot inversion tread
Staircase
Ramp w/nested curbs
Postural evaluation set
Training mirror, 3-section, portable
Treadmill Healthwalker w/rails
Low balance beam
Low parallel bars

RESISTANCE TRAINING EQUIPMENT
Quadriceps table
Quadriceps boots w/bar and collars
Dumbbell set
Grip exerciser
Rubber cable exerciser
Barbell set

TESTING AND MEASUREMENT
EQUIPMENT
Hand dynamometer
Back, leg, and chest dynamometer
Dry spirometer
Bodyweight scale
Padded table

RECREATION EQUIPMENT
Medicine ball
Table tennis table, adjustable height
    w/removable sidewalls
All-surface hockey set
Cage ball
Bowlite set
Quoit stand
Quoit, rubber, green
Quoit, rubber, yellow
Shuffleboard set

COST SUMMARY (approximate)

Remedial exercise equipment	
Stationary equipment	5476.00
Movable equipment	3579.10
Resistance training equipment	1160.70
Testing and measurement equipment	1457.10
Recreation equipment	637.70
Total	12,310.60

*Prepared by Bernard Kirschenbaum, Assistant Director, Bureau for Health and Physical Education, New York City Board of Education, November, 1974.

Index

Equipment room, 104-105; *see also* specific sports
security, 105
space requirements, 105
Equipment storage space, 171-175
Exercise rooms, 91-93

F

Fabric roof, 69
Fabric shelter; *see* Membrane structure
Facility centralization, 12
Facility conversion, 13-19
Facility costs, 12
Facility expansion, 46-47
Facility innovations, 60-82, 151-160
for swimming pools, 128-139
Facility multiuse concept, 20-26
Facility need, 30-31
Facility obsolescence, 29, 43
Facility planning; *see* Planning process
Facility purpose, interior design and, 83-84
Facility renovation, 46-47
Facility sharing, 8-12
partnership in, 12-13
Facility space requirements, 168-175
Fast track scheduling, 43
Federation of State High School Associations, 117
Figure control rooms, 91-93
Figure skating, 140
Filtration for swimming pools, 127-128
Finkelstein, Moe, 36-37
First aid, 106-108
Fitness corners, 151-153
Floating swimming pools, 128
Football equipment space, 171
Forman School, 27, 68
Fuller, R. Buckminster, 79

G

Geodesic domes, 79-82
Golf equipment space, 174
Grass surfaces, synthetic, 51, 54, 58
Gulf Breeze, Fla., school system, 11-12, 76, 78-79
Gymnasium design, 85-87; *see also* Interior design
for combative activities, 89-91
community room, 94-95
exercise rooms, 91-93
figure control rooms, 91-93
individualized boundary markers, 159-160
saunas, 93-94
space dividers, 85-86
special population facilities, 95-98
specification sources, 84
storage facilities, 87
surfacing material, 86-87, 98
turntable facilities, 159
weight training facilities, 91-93
wrestling facilities, 89-91
Gymnastics, 87-89
space requirements, 89
Gymnastics equipment, 88, 90, 178-184

H

Handicapped
building specifications and, 97-98
facilities for, 92-93
mainstreaming education for, 95
physical education for, 95, 98
pools for, 137
shower facilities for, 104
statistics, 96
terminology for, 95
Hearing defects, 96, 97
Hockey, 140; *see also* Ice arena(s)
clock, 148
locker rooms, 149
penalty box, 148
players' boxes, 148
timer's box, 148
Hofstra University, 21, 58
Houston Astrodome, 27
Hydrotherapy, 107

I

Ice arena(s), 140-143; *see also* Hockey
acoustics, 146
concessions, 150
custodial personnel, 149-150
ice making and removal, 147
kick boards, 147-148
laundry room, 149
lighting, 146
multiple use of, 143, 145
public rooms, 150
refrigeration plant, 146-147
scheduled use of, 143, 145
seating, 146
side (dasher) boards, 147-148
skate sharpening room, 148
specifications, 142-143, 145
synthetic ice for, 145, 159
year-round use, 145
Ice facilities, 140-150
Ice making, 147
Ice resurfacing machine, 148-149
Ice skate sharpening, 149
Ice skating, history of, 140
Idaho State University, 26
Indoor facilities for outdoor skills, 156-158
In-ground pools
construction materials, 126-127
finishes, 127
Interior design, 83-99; *see also* Gymnasium design
facility purpose and, 83
interest orientation and, 83
sex factor, 84-85
Intramural sports equipment space, 175

J

Japanese World's Fair, U.S. Pavilion, 60
John F. Kennedy School and Community Center, 12
Joint occupancy, 13-19

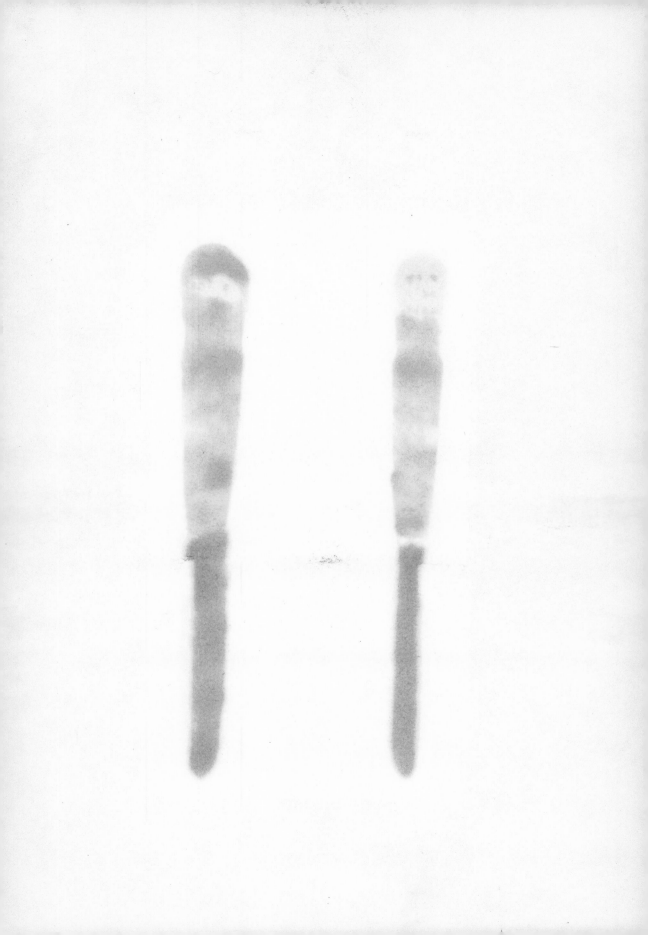